D0199963

# DISCOVER SOUTHEAST ALASKA

## WITH PACK & PADDLE

## 2nd Edition

## Margaret Piggott

WITHDRAWN

MAY 2 1 2020

UNBC Library

UNBC

LIBRARY

## The Mountaineers/Seattle

**The Mountaineers:** Organized 1906 "... *to explore, study, preserve, and enjoy the natural beauty of the Northwest.*"

© 1990 by Margaret Piggott
All rights reserved

4   3   2   1   0
5   4   3   2   1

No part of this book may be reproduced in any form, or by any electronic, mechanical, or other means, without permission in writing from the publisher.

Published by The Mountaineers
306 Second Avenue West, Seattle, Washington 98119
Published simultaneously in Canada by Douglas & McIntyre, Ltd., 1615 Venables Street, Vancouver, B.C. V5L 2H1

Manufactured in the United States of America
Edited by Jim Jenson
Cover design by Betty Watson
Book design and layout by Bridget Culligan
Cover photograph: Haines from Mount Ripinsky
Maps by: Margaret Piggott

Library of Congress Cataloguing in Publication Data

Piggott, Margaret H.
   Discover southeast Alaska with pack and paddle  /  by Margaret H. Piggott.—2nd ed.
      p.   cm.
      ISBN 0-89886-242-6
   Includes bibliographical references and index.
   1. Alaska—Description and travel—1981—Guide-books.
   2.   Trails—Alaska—Guide-books.   3. Hiking—Alaska—Guide-books.
   4. Backpacking—Alaska—Guide-books.   5. Canoes and canoeing—
   Alaska—Guide-books.   I. Title.
   F902.3.F53   1990
   917.9804′5—dc20                                          90-36104
                                                                 CIP

This book is printed on 80% recycled paper.

*To my mother*
*Who instilled in me at an early age,*
*My love for the out-of-doors.*

*To Lynn Canal Conservation*
*And all who love the mountains and the wilderness.*

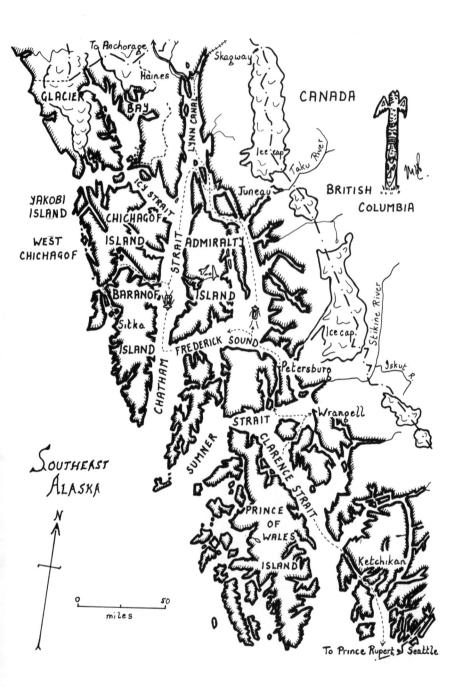

To Anchorage.
Skagway
Haines
CANADA
GLACIER
BAY
Ice cap.
Taku River
BRITISH
COLUMBIA
Juneau
YAKOBI
ISLAND
ICY STRAIT
CHICHAGOF
ISLAND
ADMIRALTY
WEST
CHICHAGOF
STRAIT
Stikine River
BARANOF
ISLAND
Sitka
Ice cap.
ISLAND
CHATHAM
FREDERICK SOUND
Iskut R.
Petersburg
Wrangell
STRAIT
SUMNER
CLARENCE STRAIT
SOUTHEAST
ALASKA
N
PRINCE
OF
WALES
ISLAND
Ketchikan
0        50
miles
To Prince Rupert & Seattle

# CONTENTS

*Upper Silvis Lake from Twin Peaks*

# FOREWORD

THE HEART of Southeast Alaska is the forests and the life they contain. The forests cover the land like a great, green mantle; huge spruce trees and hemlocks filter the light over a moss-covered floor and keep the deep snows off the forest trails so that deer can reach the beach in winter for forage and survival. The soul of Southeast Alaska is a Tlingit carving, the smallest trembling whisker on the inquisitive face of a pine marten, the gaudy iridescence of a dragonfly in flight, and the steel grey light of tidal waters before a storm. Its lifeblood is the rain and heavy snowfall, which maintains the lush greenness. Southeast Alaska is the sum of its parts. Anything taken away affects the whole, and to strip the land of its trees, valleys, and wildlife is to strip the Mona Lisa of her paint for the price it will bring.

Yet the hinterland bureaucracies and Panhandle towns (whose frontier charm draws visitors from thousands of miles) are bowing to the forces of this frantic age. Logging of the climax forests is continuing. Mining is returning to Juneau and vicinity; it already affects Skagway and may in the future change Haines. Private lands have replaced public lands where trails once existed. The wilds are becoming tamed through small-time, creeping desecrations that go unnoticed until the cumulative effect hits one like a shovel: Loran lights blink unexpectedly in the night sky, radio and telephone towers grow like mushrooms on ridgetops, newcomers come north for the fast buck and expect their home comforts to follow, and eagles are killed or maimed by trigger-happy hooligans. A valley is logged, then another, and another.

Visitors from the concrete jungle and pollution of the Lower 48 come as refugees for a summer of peace and sanity. Let's hope this refuge survives, and Alaska can remain a place of few people, bad weather, mosquitos, and large areas of unproductive space where wolves howl at sunset.

◆   ◆   ◆

While researching this book I was hopeful I might stay ahead of the bulldozer and the tailings maker, but now I am not so sure. So in the interval between writing and publication, changes in trail accessibility and condition may occur. My apologies if the data given does not reflect those changes.

Margaret H. Piggott
*Haines, Alaska*

# BREAK UP

Snow country.
Glaciers calve in this goose-weather
And these excesses of God leach the warm.

A white landscape lurking in the angles
Of a barbiturate calm.
A black frontier, keening ground beyond
The rood's shadow.
Too quick for the camera,
You linger in myth and rune.
The inanimate Basilisk.

The blind hand reaches out.
Wolves howl from their pulpit of bones,
A million years old tonight.

*Charles Lillard*

# ACKNOWLEDGMENTS

No INFORMATIONAL book can be written without help, even though all trails described here were personally inspected.

In Haines, my thanks to John Hedrick (and KHNS—FM radio) who started my computer career; to Ray Menaker for the use of his computer and help with my muddled thinking; in Skagway, Frank Norris, the National Park Service historian, was helpful on all Skagway trails and nudged me into starting the updated version of this guide. Candy Norris, Chilkoot Trail Supervisor, Canadian Parks Service, helped with the Canadian part of the trail. White Pass & Yukon Route helped with railroad access and provided me with up-to-date information. In Juneau, Judy Cooper showed me some of the best trails I had over-looked. In Sitka, Lynda Williamson and Kermit Whittemore were re-sponsible for getting me to the Sitka Causeway and were generally very helpful for other Sitka trails. Avie Fennimore helped with wheels in Wrangell. In Petersburg, Richard Sprague picked up the pieces when I broke my wrist and helped with the Kupreanof trails. Leslie and Jim Schwartz made the difference with Petersburg Creek and Raven's Roost. In Ketchikan, Bob Fernbach was a friend indeed. We explored many trails together and got lost twice—or was it three times—on one of the most interesting ones. Jim and Christa Bruce have been very supportive over the years and took me into Naha. U.S. Forest Service, Ketchikan Ranger District and Doug Campbell were immensely helpful. Without Doug's help I would not have seen many Ketchikan areas.

Lissa Fahlman, U.S. Forest Service, Petersburg Ranger District, helped me see new areas and monitored the manuscript. John Neary, Supervisor Wilderness Ranger, Admiralty NM was able to give me up-to-date information on the Admiralty Island Canoe Traverse. I would not have made it into Admiralty at all if it had not been for Ray Brown from Sequim, Washington, and his fishing vessel the *Nightwatch.* Thanks to Ric Iannolino for introducing me to Stan Price and his im-petuous bears at Pack Creek. McKie Campbell of Juneau returned me to Oliver Inlet tramway after repairs had been made. Nancy Sim-merman, formerly of Girdwood, Alaska, gave great encouragement when it was most needed—at the beginning—when rewriting a book really looks impossible.

My thanks are due to Barbara Kalen and Scott Horne of Skagway; Dan Henry, Jeannie Lombardi, and C. J. Jones of Haines; Bob Armstrong and Mary Lou King of Juneau; Mary Muller, botanist for the U.S. Forest Service, Sitka Ranger District; and Betty Adsero of Petersburg for advice and help with the manuscript. Also thanks to Chuck's Camera Clinic in Anchorage for permission to quote from their pamphlet on camera care.

Thanks also to Donna DeShazo of the Mountaineers for being so patient and waiting many years for this manuscript, and to the Alaska weather which FINALLY cooperated in the fabulous summer of 1989. I was beginning to think I had webbed feet.

# SAFETY CONSIDERATIONS

Travel in many parts of the backcountry entails unavoidable risks that every traveler assumes and must be aware of and respect. The fact that an area is described in this book is not a representation that it will be safe for you. Trips vary greatly in difficulty and in the amount and kind of preparation needed to enjoy them safely. Some routes may have changed, or conditions on them may have deteriorated since this book was written. Also, of course, conditions can change even from day to day, owing to weather and other factors. A trip that is safe in good weather or for a highly conditioned, properly equipped traveler may be completely unsafe for someone else or unsafe under adverse conditions.

You can minimize your risks by being knowledgeable, prepared, and alert. There is not space in this book for a general treatise on wilderness safety, but there are a number of good books and public courses on the subject, and you should take advantage of them to increase your knowledge. Just as important, you should always be aware of your own limitations and conditions existing when and where you are traveling. If conditions are dangerous, or if you are not prepared to deal with them safely, change your plans! It is better to have wasted a few days than to be the subject of a wilderness rescue. These warnings are not intended to keep you out of the backcountry. Many people enjoy safe trips through the backcountry every year. However, one element of the beauty, freedom, and excitement of the wilderness is the presence of risks that do not confront us at home. When you travel in the backcountry, you assume those risks. They can be met safely, but only if you exercise your own independent judgment and common sense.

—————The Mountaineers

Top: *A family on the Chilkoot Trail during the gold rush.*
Bottom: *Old wagon road to Silverbow Basin and Perseverance Mine.*
*(Photos courtesy Alaska State Library)*

# INTRODUCTION

THIS BOOK is about a land that is half the size of California and is composed of a strip of mainland and the northern half of the Alexander Archipelago. It is a coastline of shattered peaks and icefields, long, probing tidal inlets, and islands floating offshore in the copper seas of the late afternoon sun. The granite, ice-hung peaks that tourists see along the eastern coast are 8,000 to 10,000 feet high—foothills of the Saint Elias Range, which soar to 15,300 feet in Glacier Bay and 18,000 feet (Mount Saint Elias) northwest of Yakutat, 500 miles northwest of Ketchikan. What is not ice and rock is forest, muskeg, and alpine meadows. Wildlife and people are concentrated in the latter zone within a few miles of the coastline, and most of this land is administered by the U.S. Forest Service (USFS).

Southeast Alaska, despite its size, is only a small part of the whole of Alaska. Ketchikan, 900 air miles from Anchorage, is more closely allied to Seattle, 650 miles away. Road miles from Haines to Seattle are a little over 2,000, and from Prince Rupert (and Hyder) to Seattle about 1,000. The distance from Haines to the Alcan Highway by road is 160 miles, to Anchorage about 760 miles, and from Skagway to Whitehorse 110 miles. A fjorded coastline makes havoc of road mileages. It takes an hour to go the 15 miles by ferry from Haines to Skagway, and all day to run the 350 miles through Canada (and two customs posts) by road.

All other towns covered in this guide are connected either by the Alaska State ferry (the Marine Highway System) or plane. Except for Angoon and Hydaburg, the smallest Native villages have airstrips nowadays, although small retirement and fishing communities, such as Tenakee, Port Alexander, and Port Protection (not included in this guide) still require floatplane access.

## *Access by ferry and plane*

As mentioned above, Haines, Skagway, Hyder/Stewart, and Prince Rupert are connected to the Canadian interior and Lower 48 by road. The mainline ferry run by the state serves these towns and Bellingham, connecting the road heads to the major places covered in this book. Smaller ferries connect Ketchikan with communities on Prince of Wales Island, Metlakatla, and, in summer Hyder, Alaska and Stewart,

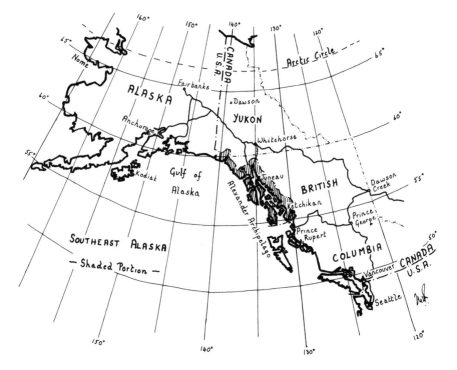

British Columbia. They also connect Juneau, Sitka, and Petersburg with communities on Chichagof and Admiralty islands. It takes about 24 hours to go from Ketchikan to Haines, but add on 17 hours for a Sitka detour. In summer the ferries are generally fully booked in advance for vehicles and staterooms and, very rarely, passengers. They offer cafeterias, showers, and drinking fountains. The crew tolerates the pitching of tents in the solarium (semi-open upper deck), but the use of stoves is not allowed. The crew would not look kindly on tent pegs hammered into the deck boards. Do not, however, pitch an un-pegged tent too far aft. It may fly overboard as soon as the ship moves away from the dock. There is an extra charge for large carry-on items, such as canoes, kayaks, and bicycles.

Jet planes fly into Juneau, Sitka, Ketchikan, Wrangell, and Petersburg, weather permitting; and smaller floatplanes or wheeled planes fly into backcountry and to the villages. Weather is a big factor in Alaska, and even in the summer a visitor can get an unplanned stop-over. So plan to take two to three days extra food when flying into a re-mote cabin.

# *Flora*

Virgin rain forests have a spacious cathedrallike quality with light shafting among huge trees, and moss-covered floors smothered in places with Canadian dogwood (CORNUS CANADENSIS). The forests of the Alaska Panhandle are composed mainly of western hemlock and Sitka spruce. Mountain hemlock is found throughout the forests, but is more noticeable at high elevations. An inland variety of the lodgepole pine (PINUS CONTORTA var. LATIFOLIA) is a tall, straight tree, found in mixed stands on the slopes over the Chilkat Valley and above Skagway. Shore pine (PINUS CONTORTA var. CONTORTA), intolerant of shade, is found on the edges of the forest in natural open areas, often growing twisted and low to the ground. The fragrant red cedar (canoe cedar) is native to Ketchikan, Petersburg, and Prince of Wales Island; and Alaska cedar (yellow cedar) is found in groves throughout Southeast Alaska, especially mixed with lodgepole pines in muskegs and open areas. Huge cottonwoods, along with giant spruce, are the nesting and perching favorites of bald eagles. They are found in the glacial outwash rivers of the upper Lynn Canal. Red alder, Sitka alder, and various willows also exist here as large shrubs or small trees.

The understory is composed of blueberry, highbush cranberry, salmonberry, huckleberry, serviceberry, rusty menziesia, and others. The floor of undisturbed forests is composed of mosses, lichens, liverworts, and the ground dogwood. Skunk cabbage (arum family) is found in muddy places on the forest floor, and often in the middle of wet trails. In spring the plant is pale yellow, and the roots are occasionally dug up by bears. Later in the year, the skunk cabbage is noted for its coarse green leaves and huge size.

Slide alder, or "octopus brush" (courtesy the Kalens, Skagway) takes over on avalanche routes and active rock gullies and where forest gives way to semi-alpine in the northern Lynn Canal (for example, A. B. Mountain). The alder is a battle to get through unless the path is cleared every two to three years, although this is often the place the piercing whistle of the hoary marmot is heard. Learn to recognize the devil's club (ECHINOPAX HORRIDUM). It is a ubiquitous "don't touch" plant, whose large, umbrellalike leaves grow on long, spiny stalks that sometimes reach a height of 10 feet. In fall, vertical clusters of red berries ripen in the center of the plant, and the leaves turn a radiant golden brown. It is beautiful and highly photogenic, but avoid contact at all costs. Fine barbs penetrate the skin and will stay for a week or

more. On steep slopes wear leather gloves if possible. (Murphy's Law dictates that the one plant on hand that will save the hiker when a slip occurs is ECHINOPAX HORRIDUM!)

On broad, gentle-sloped low ridgetops, and poorly drained flat areas, the flow of forest falters. Small, stunted pines and cedars seem to hover nervously around the edge of the clearing and advance tentatively into the open, seeking a balance between a desire for light and a dislike for waterlogged soils. These peat bog forest clearings, called "muskegs," may be a few yards or several miles across. Heathers (including Labrador tea), hardy grasses, blueberries, nagoon berries, bog cranberries, bog cotton, and many species of flowers, such as shooting stars, pond lilies, bog candle, hooded lady's tresses and round-leafed orchis grow in small groups. Also, watch for the scintillating, minuscule plant kingdom found in wet places, sundew (DROSERA ROTUNDIFOLIA and ANGELICA): tiny insectivorous plants shaped like pincushions. The leaves are covered with sticky barbs to entrap small flies, and on dew-laden mornings they sparkle like jewels. Another insectivorous plant found in wet places is the bog violet or butterwort (PINGUICULA VULGARIS). The blue flower is violetlike, but has pale green, waxy leaves that entrap insects when they alight by curling over and secreting digestive juices.

The alpine zone is found at about 2,200 to 2,500 feet, where the trees diminish in size and then disappear altogether as heathers, grasses, mosses, lichens, and certain flower groups gain the ascendancy. Mountain hemlocks become dwarf hemlocks and form impenetrable masses. Luckily for those trying to find a way into the clear, these thickets usually appear only in clumps, although they do present a problem in some Ketchikan alpine areas. Common juniper is also found as a prostrate shrub at these elevations. Alpine country is the land of wild flower gardens where one species often forms a single-colored carpet once spring snows have melted. Lupines grow in profusion and brilliant pink mats of moss campion throw a splash of color on rock outcrops. Jacob's ladder, cranesbill (wild geranium), mountain avens (DRYAS OCTOPETALA), forget-me-nots (borage family and the Alaska State flower), and the small, shy, deep-blue glaucous gentian are all found at these altitudes. Be sensitive toward these fragile meadows; do not pick flowers, and pitch camp only on the heaths and coarse grasses. Even common varieties took years to establish themselves in this harsh environment.

Opposite top: *Gastineau Channel from Mount Jumbo.* Opposite bottom: *Ducks near Petersburg. (Photo by R. T. Wallen)*

A common ground cover of semi-alpine and alpine country is the deer cabbage (FAURIA CRISTA-GALLI), which possesses a small white flower. In the fall, the leaves turn the mountains golden yellow above the treeline, but when the FAURIA finally dies, it makes a slippery footing on steep slopes.

There are many edible plants in Southeast Alaska, but the most obvious, such as the sea-beach sandwort (sea-purslane) and goose tongue, are succulent beach greens found close to, or below the high tide level. Strawberries are also often seen among the beach rocks. Look for the blue bell-like flowers of beach mertensia (sea lungwort), which hugs the ground and radiates outwards like the spokes of a wheel. One of the small yellow-flowered potentillas (a cinquefoil) grows within the intertidal zone. (Beach campers beware—don't be taken in by these pretty flowers. Look around for other evidence of the high tide mark before pitching a tent and committing the group for the night.) Among hundreds of other varieties in Southeast Alaska, purple fields of fireweed give a blaze of color to open meadows, road edges, and beach areas.

# *Wildlife*

No matter how beautiful the wilderness is, it is nothing without its wildlife. In the Alaska Panhandle many animals that are not on the archipelago prevail on the mainland, for example, red foxes, coyotes, wolverines, lynx, snowshoe hares, hoary marmots, porcupines, and Dall's sheep (although marmots are commonly heard, and porcupines sometimes seen on Douglas Island). Moose are found on large rivers, such as the Unuk, Stikine, Taku and Chilkat, which connect to the Interior. Wolves, an embattled species because of their conflicts with hunters, are distributed throughout Alaska except for "the ABC islands" (Admiralty, Baranof, and Chichagof). Mountain goats may be seen on cliffs in Glacier Bay, on the Chilkoot Pass, on high peaks above Haines, Skagway, and Juneau. Some have been introduced onto the summit of Mount Juneau. The forest quiet is often disturbed by the "chip-chip-chip" alarm call of red squirrels. Martens, mice, beavers, mink, river otters and short-tailed weasels (ermine) are found almost anywhere.

Show respect for the mice, squirrels, and martens. Those innocent, diminutive, and bewitching creatures will steal unattended food from careless campers and can ruin a trip. Food should always be hung in cabins or outside in a tree. Mink have been known to take fish being cleaned in the semi-dark, lying inches away from campers. Porcupines like salt and will nibble on outhouse seats as well as tree bark. Their penchant for chewing through old tires on abandoned cars is not as well known, but could be a source of embarrassment to anyone leaving a car in the vicinity of a rubber-addicted porcupine.

Humpback whales are seen in Frederick Sound, Stephens Passage, and Sumner Strait and from the beach in Lynn Canal. Watch for the vertical mushroom-shaped blows as they surface and the huge white-streaked T-shaped flukes as they dive. Killer whales, recognized by their vertical dorsal fin, are occasionally seen in groups, Dall porpoises are commonly seen playing tag with speeding vessels, and harbor porpoises blow with a sigh as they surface in quiet inlets and sheltered

*Red fox*

bays. Sea lions follow the herring north in spring and perform a water ballet under the harbor floats in Auke Bay and in Lutak Inlet near Haines. Wheeling white clouds of gulls tag along to pick up the herring pieces.

This nation's emblem, the bald eagle, is common throughout the coastal islands and mainland, especially over tidal waters and salmon streams. In fact, the ubiquity of this magnificent raptor is a source of pride to Southeast Alaskans, and many share the pleasure of watching its intimate life habits though the kitchen window while completing household chores. Sightings are made frequently from ferries and tour ships, much to the joy of visitors. Those with a real interest in Alaskan birds of prey, including hawks and owls, should visit the Raptor Center in Sitka.

The Panhandle would lose its sparkle without ravens—the gregarious, noisy, and unkempt clowns seen within the confines of most towns and villages. They turn somersaults in the air, then make the onlooker gulp by dropping like a stone out of sight. They banter and cajole and hurl obscenities at passing boats. Their rich repertoire of honks, gurgles, clicks, and liquid bell-like tones fill the air with staccato sound. The raven has been deified by the Tlingit Indians and other Northwest Coast tribes. It fully deserves such an honor.

In spring when the cottonwood's sweet fragrance pervades the atmosphere, varied thrushes sketch a sound profile mornings and evenings, with single, quavering, flutelike whistles repeated in different keys. Swainson's thrushes sing ascending carillons, wrens chatter and sing at the same time, and the hermit thrush sings the first bar of Beethoven's Eighth Symphony. Small birds enliven the bushes with their own rapid fire "chee-chee" notes. At alpine elevations, ptarmigan tell the hiker to "go-baaakk, go-baaakkk," and males retain their white winter plumage longer than the females to draw attention away from the nesting mate. In high ridge country hikers can be surprised by sudden appearances of hummingbirds attracted by their brightly colored clothing or packs. Many, many more birds of the sea, uplands, forests, and lakes—swans, geese, bay and harbor ducks, predatory kestrels and merlins, kingfishers, woodpeckers, and dippers—add their sound and color to the scene, when wintering, nesting, or just passing through.

No wilderness experience is complete without the howling of red-throated loons. Their evening spine-tingling calls slide down the atonal scale like the wail of banshees before a wake. A second theme, a burbling, rising laughter, evokes scenes from Macbeth. Once heard, these cries will never be confused with the falsetto-tremolo call of the common loon. Despite the bloodcurdling sound, the red-throated loons are wary of people. They flush off the water when approached and are then recognizable by a rhythmic quacking in the air. (By contrast, common loons yodel with resonant voices on the wing and in the water, but are also shy nowadays in popular areas. They no longer show the curiosity towards kayakers that they have in years past.) These magnificent birds combine with wolves as eloquent, self-appointed spokesmen for wilderness. When their voices are stilled, the wilderness my generation has known has died.

For comments about bears, see "Safety" below.

## FISHING

Many people hike the trails summer and winter to fish. Be sure to obtain a license and read the regulations for the area. Regulations can be picked up at the ferry terminals and visitor center in Haines, in sporting goods stores, and State of Alaska Fish and Game offices.

# *Weather*

Come to Southeast Alaska expecting to get wet, so if it doesn't rain, it will be a pleasant surprise. Ketchikan gets almost 160 inches, the Juneau area varies depending on one's location—the town gets about 90 inches, the Valley a lot less (53 inches). Sitka gets 96 inches, Haines 47 inches, and Skagway 26 inches. There is less precipitation in the summer than in the winter, the wettest month being October. Rain has its advantages. The glacial ice is bluer, and the low cloud tendrils very photogenic. After the rain the birds sing. The mountains, glaciers, tidal inlets glisten white and blue and are half hidden behind dissipating clouds. This is the time the mountains seem close and tall and greater than life size. So bring a raincoat and enjoy the rain.

The best summer months seem to be May and June; sunny days with temperatures in the 70s and 80s are possible. Otherwise expect temperatures in the 50s. The sunniest winter months are January and February although expect low temperatures (to zero and below) and high winds in Juneau, Haines, and Skagway. However, a warm current parallels the coastline resulting in a temperate climate overall for coastal Alaska. In winter, expect a 20- to 30-degree drop in temperatures when going over the Coast Range into the Interior.

Coastal ice and the face of any glacier will also create colder conditions by as much as 20 degrees. Even on a warm day be sure to take warm clothing when visiting a glacier.

Never trust the weather. Expect it to change!

# *Safety*

## THE TEN ESSENTIALS

The Mountaineers have compiled a list of Ten Essentials considered necessary for survival. These should be taken on any hike of moderate length.

**1. Extra food.** Candy, nuts, or other high-energy food stuffed into a rucksack.

**2. Extra clothing.** Even on hot days take extra clothing. An Alaskan walk can start with temperatures in the 70s and end with heavy snow or driving sleet on the high ridgetops. Always take a hat (much of the body's heat loss is through the head) and gloves. Also long pants and wool or polypropylene sweater, and wind- or waterproof pants and jacket should all be worn or put in the pack. Take waterproof wear for forest walks—even on good days after a rainfall the wet brush can soak a person in minutes. On high alpine ridges, quick drying windproof shell over wool is the best combination. Be sure to wear wool or polypropylene socks.

**3. Map; 4. Compass.** No one is immune to getting lost. Alaskan berrypickers have wandered a few yards off a major highway close to their homes and spent a night out in the bush. Map and compass and a knowledge of orienteering would set travelers straight in minutes (see "Getting Lost" below).

**5. Matches; 6. Firestarter.** Extra warmth from a fire can be a lifesaver in cold, wet conditions. Most searches in Alaska are done from the air, and smoke is the best way to signal position in heavily forested terrain. Place matches in a watertight container (kitchen matches in ziplock bags or in plastic screw-top bottles). Lighters make a good secondary source of fire, but do not leave watertight matches behind. A firestarter is often necessary in addition to matches or lighter, especially if the fuel is wet. Candles make good firestarters. Pitch taken from a spruce tree or low dead branches will work, too. Or carry dry birch bark or buy a commercial starter. In heavy rain where cedars grow use the underside bark of fallen trees.

**7. Knife; 8. First aid kit; 9. Flashlight.** These items are self-explanatory. A flashlight is needed when least expected—for signaling or to light the way for a late return. Take extra batteries.

**10. Sunglasses.** Eye protection is important when traveling on

*The aftermath of a bottomless boghole*

snow in summer or winter or for crossing open water. Snowblindness is painful, debilitating, and potentially dangerous to the eyes.

## OTHER NECESSITIES

On most non-boardwalk forest trails, rubber fishing boots that extend to mid-calf and have lug soles ("Ketchikan sneakers") are the best form of footwear. Wear sturdy hiking or climbing boots for alpine trips. An ice ax is needed for steep snow slopes.

Strong twine (nylon clothesline is best), whistle, and signal mirror are important extras. Also take a space blanket for emergencies, and include nylon cord with snowshoes in case of trouble with bindings. Insect repellent makes life a lot easier in the bush. Sunscreen is important, especially for snow hiking days. Small brush trimmers are useful for poorly maintained trails. Sometimes surveyor's tape is useful for marking a route where it emerges into alpine country or a muskeg; but remove the tape on the return so as not to confuse others who come after. (Too much brightly colored tape in the woods is a problem, also.)

Compulsive hikers should have the Ten Essentials, camera, and binoculars in a pack always ready to go. Then no time is wasted when the good weather day arrives.

## BEAR TROUBLE?

Alaska brown bears are larger than, but otherwise identical to, the grizzly (URSUS ARCTOS HORRIBILIS), which is indigenous to the western United States and Canada. Black bears (URSUS AMERICANUS) have many color phases, from cinnamon to the rare blue glacial bear, and lack the massive size and hump of the brown bear. Both species range the mainland. Brown bears are found on the ABC islands, and black bears live on the islands south of Frederick Sound. Both species demand respect from all who go into the woods, as their behavior is unpredictable and dangerous. If common sense and care are exercised, most direct confrontations with bears can be avoided.

A loud (not shrill) whistle will deter bears that are merely curious and not already annoyed or cornered. (A shrill whistle may sound too much like a marmot to a bear.) Attach a bell to boots or pack, talk loudly, or shake pebbles in a can to warn most bears of a person's presence, and—most important—give a mother bear a chance to retreat with her cubs to a safe distance. Mothballs are sometimes carried by

Opposite top: *Alaska brown bear.* Opposite bottom: *Blueberries.*

campers because they have a reputation of discouraging bears; if nothing else they mask the odor of food.

Keep food well away from tent and kayaks; it is best hung in a tree, 12 feet off the ground at least 100 feet away. Do not bury cans. Wash them and carry them out. Fish has a strong odor and is highly attractive to bears, so be sure fish is kept away from boats and camp. Failing this, be sure that boats are thoroughly cleaned to get rid of any smells. Do not camp on bear trails. If a bear is on the trail, give it the right-of-way! Do not approach a bear too closely, even for photographs. Use a high-powered telephoto lens instead, or retain the memory and forget the picture.

Bears habituated to humans (so-called tame bears) are NOT TAME. They are deadly. They have lost their fear of people and associate humans with food. These are the garbage bears, the ones who have been given handouts by people (which incidentally is illegal). Confrontations may occur in Pack Creek on Admiralty Island (please refer to the USFS literature) or any place where they have had close contact with humans over a period of time. Garbage bears may be seen in spring in Juneau. Avoid them. Do not approach closely. Habituated bears are rarely seen far from human habitation.

Human beings are the interlopers in Alaskan backcountry, and an understanding and sensitivity toward the rights of bears will help save both bear and human lives. Although carrying a gun is an individual decision, it includes responsibilities toward others in the woods. Bear encounters are rare, and a gun's efficacy in the hands of a non-expert is debatable. A wounded bear is doubly dangerous to other hikers.

In the remote chance of a bear charge, stand still. Do not run, because bears often bluff but will chase fleeing prey. If the confrontation is with a brown bear and a tree is handy, back slowly to the tree, dropping a hat or pack to distract the bear, and climb up at least 15 feet. (Be warned. Black bears, unlike the Alaskan brown bears, climb trees.) If caught on the ground face down, bring knees to chest, protect the back of the neck with the hands, and play dead.

Visitors from "Outside" who do not venture onto any trail because of a fear of bears should note these animals are practically never seen on well-used trails close to towns. Most bears will avoid humans, and it is safer to walk in Alaskan backcountry than to walk a street in a major American city. Do not carry smelly food, stay away from tidal flats and rivers during spawning season, and a bear sighting probably will be avoided.

And don't forget. Moose are dangerous, too. Do not get too close to a mother with her young. Treat all moose with respect, and keep your distance.

# GETTING LOST

Getting lost is easy, and everyone does it at some time or another. It is part of the initiation. The big thing is to have the guts to admit being lost and immediately attempt to retrace the way back to the original route.

Sudden deteriorating weather conditions are probably the most common cause of missing the way, particularly in alpine regions. If visibility worsens, take immediate bearings of dominant features in the direction of travel. Re-check with the map. If fog envelopes the party, have a member of the group walk ahead, but remain in sight. The person setting the compass course can then line the lead hiker on the correct course, calling directions if the person strays to the right or to the left.

Many of the trails described here, which give access onto alpine ridges, are not developed enough to be obvious once the trees are left behind. Hikers should look back at the trail on the way in, otherwise they may spend the night on top. Never try shortcuts off a mountain (particularly Mount Juneau, A. B. Mountain in Skagway, Mount Ripinsky in Haines) especially in poor weather or gathering darkness. It is, in the long run, quicker and safer to return by the trail or route of access.

Often in spring snows the trail tread is lost; it can disappear totally in deep woods unless care is taken to watch for tree blazes and markers. Stay alert and keep looking back to remember the return route.

A subalpine ridge with a nebulous trail sometimes presents a route-finding challenge. If the drop becomes steeper than expected, consider the possibility that the party has wandered onto the steep side of the ridge and not the ridge end. (This is when a compass becomes useful.) To avoid getting "cliff hung" climb back onto the ridge. Have the strength of mind to admit the mistake and stop descending.

If weather has deteriorated, and the party feels irrevocably lost, find a sheltered place; set up a tarp or tent and build a fire. Wait for the weather to improve before moving again. Be alert to signs of hypothermia in yourself and other party members. Signal distress by grouping signals into threes: three closely grouped fires on a wilderness beach would prompt a passing boat to investigate, or repetitions of three gunshots or three blasts on a whistle.

# HYPOTHERMIA

Hypothermia, the prime killer of outdoor recreationists, is more common than many people realize. Hypothermia is a drop in body temperature due to cold or wet conditions and/or fatigue. It can be recognized by slowing of pace, clumsiness, disorientation, apathy, and irrational behavior. As soon as any member of the party appears to be getting irreversibly cold, stop. Find a sheltered spot (retreat into trees, if at all possible) and build a fire. Do not give food or drink if the victim is not fully rational or conscious. Do not give alcohol under any circumstances. If the victim is wet, insist that they don dry clothing. Failing that, wrap the cold person in a plastic tarp or garbage bag to create a vapor barrier, which will reduce heat loss due to evaporation. If a sleeping bag, tent, or space blanket is available, use them, and insulate the victim from the ground. (Warm the sleeping bag beforehand or get into the bag with patient. A sleeping bag insulates; it will not raise the victim's body temperature on its own.) Concentrate on warming the core areas, such as the head, chest, groin, and armpits. Keep the extremities cool. Do not leave the patient alone.

Wind chill is also a killer. Subtract one degree in temperature per mile an hour in wind speed and plan accordingly.

## GIARDIASIS

GIARDIA LAMBLIA is a waterborne parasite, which can be carried in cyst form by all mammals, including dogs and humans. It is found in some Alaskan streams and lakes that have been polluted by mammal feces. Drinking tainted water brings on symptoms of abdominal pain, bloating, excessive gas, and diarrhea usually within 8 to 10 days. Any water source can be contaminated, including clear running streams. Poor sanitary practices may also allow GIARDIA to be passed on between people. Hikers are advised to carry their own water, or boil water for one minute, or use chlorine or iodine and let stand for 30 minutes if the water is turbid or cold. Most filters are inadequate, unless designed specifically for this purpose; filtration of less than five micrometers is needed to eliminate the parasite.

People can help keep waterborne diseases clear of lakes and river and stream systems by keeping their dogs under control and out of water courses. Campers should carry a collapsible bucket and not wash directly in a stream or lake. If toilets are provided, use them; if not, dig a hole at least 100 feet from water and cover well afterwards.

# *Backcountry conditions*

When venturing into backcountry take a friend or go with a group. (In Juneau contact the parks and recreation department to find out about city-sponsored hikes.) Be sure someone at home knows the day's plan and the time of return. Plan ahead. Decide beforehand when the party must turn back, whether the objective has been reached or not. Before leaving, day hikers should ask themselves if they can survive the night out of doors given the current time of year.

## AVALANCHES

Some of the deep valley routes described are subject to avalanches during winter and early spring. Especially vulnerable are those close to the downtown area of Juneau, the Chilkoot Trail, and the Blue Lake road east of Sitka. Inquire of locals or the parks and recreation department in Juneau, the U.S. Forest Service (USFS) in Sitka, and the National Park Service (NPS) in Skagway, if unsure of the status of any of these trails. High ridges are also subject to cornicing (overhanging snow), which may collapse without warning. Stay away from snow edges and remain behind cracks on ridge edges.

## GLACIERS

Some of the described trails give access to glaciers. Hikers are warned not to wander onto the neve unless they have the equipment and knowledge of glacier travel. The neve is permanent snow, which conceals crevasses (deep cracks in the ice) and forms snow bridges, many of which are unsafe. Ice caves and seracs (ice pinnacles) are fun to look at, but they can collapse suddenly causing injury or death.

## WET BOARDS AND SPRING SNOW

Be wary of wet and icy puncheon, boardwalk, fallen trees, or any boards underfoot. I broke a wrist after slipping on wet boardwalk while working on this book, and a friend did the same thing on a sloping boardwalk near Juneau. Petersburg and Sitka ranger districts use chicken wire to hold unwary feet, other districts and agencies use slats or build the boardwalks as staircases. Rarely, puncheon is laid down and a tread made of cedar chips, which provides safe walking for years.

Be cautious of boardwalks in thawing snow. Holes develop over the steps and edges of the board, and one can fall in, or fall off, the boardwalk. It is best to stay completely clear of the boards at these times. (At higher elevations expect the same problem stepping off rock onto spring snow or stepping onto a buried tree. Natural thin-roofed snowcaves often exist in these places.)

## RIVER CROSSINGS

Although no swift river crossings are called for in the trails described, it is possible that awkward river confrontations will take place because of washed-out bridges.

Always treat rivers with respect; their dangers are not apparent at

first sight. On hot days cross glacial rivers during the morning. With melting snow they can become raging torrents by afternoon. Beware of ice chunks and rolling rocks, which can knock the unwary off their feet. In murky glacial water the leader should probe the bottom for deep holes.

To cross safely, remember a few basic rules:

**1.** Look for the widest place where current speed and depth are diminished, or look for braided streams.

**2.** In deep rivers, take off socks and put boots back on to allow firm footing.

**3.** Undo pack waistband.

**4.** Use a long stick for counterbalance, or link hands. Sometimes a handline or a belay with a rope is necessary.

**5.** Keep feet apart and face upcurrent, if difficulty occurs.

**6.** Use the stick to probe for holes.

**7.** Measure the party's ability to cross by its weakest member.

# Backcountry travel

## CABINS

Permits must be obtained from the USFS (or the state, for Oliver Inlet) before using a cabin. A fee is levied for maintenance costs. (Some cabins in the Juneau area may be used during the day without a permit.) Most cabins have adequate stoves, wood on hand, axes, and brooms to clean the cabin after use. Do not leave food behind. It attracts bears and mice. Bears have been known to break through windows to get to food and then demolish the interior trying to get out again. Please latch the door when you leave.

At some cabins the USFS leaves rowboats. Please be sure to bring the boat out of the water and turn it upside down. Towards the end of the season it is especially important to get the boat well above the waterline because of freezing temperatures.

## VANDALISM

Please respect all private and public property found in the back-country. Many of the backcountry improvements were done by citi-

*Slippery boardwalk, Kupreanof Loop*

*The Chilkat Mountains and Chilkat River Estuary from Mount Riley*

zens and local interest groups, and many of the cabins were built by voluntary labor. Do not forget that damage done to USFS, state, or NPS property is taking money out of the public's pocket. Private cabins have not been identified to discourage vandalism. In the past, some cabins have been instrumental in saving the lives of lost hunters and hikers. The next life saved may be yours.

## TENT CAMPING

Always take a rainproof flysheet for the tent. Plastic garbage bags are useful for keeping the pack and other items dry. Very fine insect netting for doorways to keep out no-see-ums as well as mosquitos and white socks is also advisable. At all camps please pack out garbage and leave wood for others. (Cut only dead or downed trees.) Use the fire rings already in place; otherwise make your own ring out of stones before lighting a fire. Be sure the fire is completely out—douse it well with water when the party leaves. Dead wood is scarce at subalpine altitudes so take cooking stoves to high-level camps. Where there is no toilet, dig a hole far away from streams and lakes, and cover well after-wards.

Do not bury cans; this practice endangers future campers. A bear may investigate a cache of buried cans on which another party, igno-rant of its existence, has set up camp.

PLEASE PACK OUT ALL GARBAGE whether going out for the day or the week!

## CAMERAS

The Panhandle is a place where the rain comes down in buckets and can sink a small boat in hours. Always keep camera, binoculars, and maps in strong ziplock bags, or any waterproof container. Do not leave an unprotected camera in the bottom of a boat or tent. If the camera gets properly submersed, take out the film and batteries. Place the film into its container with fresh water and let the developers know what has happened. If possible, separate the lens from the body and wrap the parts in warmed towels to draw out the moisture. If still wet, seal them in ziplock bags, squeezing out as much air as possible. Keep it sealed until delivering them to the repair shop. If the camera lands in sea water, rinse it first in fresh water, then follow the same procedure.

## CANOEING

The term "canoe" is used in this book to mean either a canoe or kayak. Canoes can be transported by the Alaska State Marine Highway for a small fee. Folding kayaks are less expensive and more convenient for air charter; few planes are equipped to handle the non-folding type.

Canoeists going out onto open waters should take the following precautions:

◆ Wear Coast Guard-approved life jackets at all times when on the wa-ter. If traveling after dark, be sure to have adequate lighting. All boats should have a repair kit, painters, extra paddle, spray cover, and ade-quate flotation. Clothing and perishable food should be well sealed in plastic bags. Also make sure that sealed matches, firestarter, a knife, whistle, and some candy or nuts are on the person at all times when paddling.

◆ Practice adequate rescue techniques in familiar water with other members of the party before beginning a trip. Rescue after an upset must be fast to avoid the onset of hypothermia; Alaskan waters, even in the summer, are cold. Exposure suits are bulky but lifesavers in cold waters—and they do make good pillows! Take one along, but practice putting it on in the water before leaving on the expedition. If all else fails, a wet suit is insurance against hypothermia, but these are not that comfortable to wear for extended periods.

◆ When doing extended paddle trips over large open stretches of water, there should never be a time crunch. Plan extra days for sudden weather changes. People who try to outwit the weather and rush home have paid with their lives. Don't rush things! Go for a walk in the rain and wind instead, or play cards in the tents and wait for safer crossing conditions.

◆ Always have a current, local tide table on hand. These can be obtained free of charge at most sporting goods stores in Southeast Alaska. Be sure to bring the boats well above the high tide mark before camping for the night. Tides can fluctuate by as much as 20 feet in this area. Beware of large fast-moving cruise ships. Their wake can also cause unexpected tidal fluctuations. Do not leave fish or smelly food in or close to the boats, since this will attract bears.

## COMMUNICATIONS

Many community FM radio stations put listener personals or "muskeg messages" over the air as a public service to those without a phone. KRBD serves Ketchikan and many Prince of Wales Island com-

*Sitka black-tailed deer (Photo by R. T. Wallen)*

munities; KSTK Wrangell; KFSK Petersburg; KCAW Sitka, Angoon, and
Kake; KTOO Juneau, Hoonah, and Gustavus; and KHNS Haines, Klukwan, and Skagway.

## LAND ADMINISTRATION

The USFS administers most of the land in Southeast Alaska, including Admiralty Island National Monument. Some of the land around the
towns has come under state selection and has been given to city and
borough administrations for development. The NPS administers Glacier Bay, the Chilkoot Trail, part of Skagway, and a small historical park
in Sitka. The northwestern part of Southeast Alaska is state land.

# *How to use this book*

This guide follows the ferry from north to south, taking in only
the major towns for the present. The "milk run" through Tenakee, Pel-
ican, Kasaan, etc., may come later, although trails are not well developed in the villages. Once a town is reached, almost all the trails
described are accessible by car, bicycle, public transportation, or foot.
The most notable exceptions are those on Kupreanof Island (Petersburg), Naha River (Ketchikan), and the Airport Causeway (Sitka).

*Alaska's Panhandle is rich in water birds. (Photo by R. T. Wallen)*

## INFORMATION BLOCKS

Times and distances are one way, unless stated. Elevation gain is the total height climbed going both in and out and does not necessarily reflect the height of the destination. Unless otherwise stated extended trips reflect the total one-way time, distance, and elevation gain from car park, city center or boat landing.

Times are somewhat arbitrary. A lot depends on the priorities of the participant. The younger ones need to get to the top NOW, and the older ones like to look at the flowers or take photographs. There is a lot of difference in those times; so use the approximations given as a guide only. My advice is to decide beforehand roughly how long the day should be and turn back about the halfway point whether the objective has been reached or not.

Mileposts and car mileages are used to give distances to trailheads. The two often differ, however. Mileposts get moved over the years, or the roads are shortened through improvements, so be prepared for inconsistencies, especially in the Juneau area.

## DIFFICULTY RATINGS

*Easy*—wide, well-graded route, which generally can be done in tennis shoes; appropriate for older people.

*Moderate*—usually forest trails, no more than 1,800 feet of elevation gain. There may be some difficult footing; these trails are often wet, so use waterproof boots.

*Strenuous*—alpine altitudes and steep trails. Wear good hiking or climbing boots. An ice ax may be necessary on steep slopes. These routes are for experienced hikers who understand their limitations in unfamiliar territory. Most of these trails go above the tree line and are subject to the vagaries of Alaska weather at high altitudes.

Expect the trails to change. Flagging comes and goes. Helpful and unhelpful signs appear, disappear, and reappear. Brush grows up over the years, beavers flood the countryside, winter storms blow over trees, many feet make bottomless bogholes of the duff, the mountain slides, or someone comes in and builds a stretch of boardwalk, a road, a mine, or a town over the trail site. Yes, they change, and it sometimes makes backcountry travel a challenge.

## MAPS

It is advisable to have a local topographic map and compass on hand when walking in the woods, even on a trail. When spring snow is on the ground a hiker will lose the trail at some time or another. Those in alpine country should also have a map with them because the weather can change quickly, reducing visibility. It also gives the traveler a lot of interesting information about the terrain. All maps are either topographic quadrangles or unless stated charts. The 1:63,360 series is 1 mile to an inch, the 1:250,000 is 4 miles to the inch, and 1:24,000 is 1 mile to 2.6 inches.

The difference between true north and magnetic north is known as *declination*. The USGS topographic maps indicate the declination to the nearest degree. In Southeast Alaska the declination is between 28 and 31 east of true north and must be taken into account when using a compass. An easy way to take a compass bearing is to set the needle on the declination, then read from true north, south, etc. But, like everything, it should be practiced first before an emergency occurs. Before going out, get help from friends or check the library for reference material.

The sketch maps in this book are drawn in such a way as to give useful information and are not necessarily to scale; thus mileages have not been given. All hikers should take along appropriate USGS topographic maps. They are advised to purchase the maps for each area they plan to visit before they travel to Southeast Alaska. Local topographic maps and charts can usually be obtained in each town, but the traveler should not depend on this. In the larger towns inquire at stores selling marine equipment.

◆  ◆  ◆

All the warnings given above are not meant to dampen the enthusiasm of the wilderness explorer. The big thing is to forestall trouble by planning ahead, by being willing to turn back when conditions get difficult or dangerous (and recognizing these conditions exist in the first place) and by using common sense. A wilderness experience is one to be enjoyed, and most times it is. The rewards of walking and camping in backcountry are many, although the experience can be both ennobling and humbling.

*Please carry out all garbage! And never trust the weather!*

# SKAGWAY

SKAGWAY can be reached by road from Whitehorse, Yukon Territory, 110 miles away. It is the northern terminus of the Alaska Marine Highway in Southeast Alaska and is located at the head of a long fjord at the northern end of Lynn Canal, in a narrow valley locked within mountain walls 4,000 to 6,000 feet high. In spring, Skagway is redolent with fresh cottonwood shoots, and in autumn, the valley and lower mountain birch trees shimmer gold in stark contrast to the first dusting of snow on the mountain tops. In winter the wind h-o-o-o-w-w-ls, the nights are long, the peaks are stark and cold, very aloof, and the valleys deep purple. This is the time the townsfolk find their skates and hike up to Lower Dewey Lake for a day of fun or carry their skis to the White Pass summit and beyond to Fraser and Log Cabin.

Skagway played a crucial role in the Klondike gold rush during the hectic years of 1897 and 1898. It was a gathering point for stampeders bound for the Chilkoot Trail, the gateway through the coastal range into Canada's interior and the Yukon River headwaters. The White Pass & Yukon Railroad (WP&YR), built in 1900 to connect Skagway with Whitehorse, diminished the importance of the Chilkoot Trail as a route inland, although by then the rush was over. Skagway today is a modern town, but the false-fronted buildings, saloons, and wooden boardwalks retain a historical ambience. Now with the influence of the Klondike Gold Rush National Historical Park, the Chilkoot is reasserting its former importance, this time as a mecca to those who wish to relive the past and have heard of the legendary beauty of the coastal range.

Visitors to Skagway should visit the National Park Service (NPS) Visitor Center on Second and Broadway (the old railroad depot) for information on the history of the area and up-to-date information on the trails. The WP&YR closed in 1982, but is again open and operating between Skagway and Fraser, and Fraser and Bennett. Hikers should use the trains when they are operating; at other times, they walk the railroad tracks at their own risk.

Anyone visiting or hiking in the area will appreciate the stay more if they do some reading beforehand to acquaint themselves with the history and atmosphere of the town and two valleys.

# CHILKOOT TRAIL
## S1

**TIME:** allow 3–5 days
**DISTANCE:** 33 miles
**ELEVATION GAIN:** northbound 4,900 feet; southbound 2,750 feet
**RATING:** strenuous
**ACCESS:** car; WP&YR and boat from Bennett
**TYPE:** historical, coastal and boreal forest, alpine
       winter ski run from Log Cabin to Bennett
**MAPS:** Skagway B-1 and C-1, 1 inch:1 mile; White Pass 104M/11 East;
       Lake Homan 104M/14 East; and Tutshi Lake 104M/15 West, 1.25
       inch:1 mile.
Avalanche danger April to late June; foul weather likely
Customs clearance is mandatory

The great attraction of the Chilkoot Trail is its gold rush history between 1897 and 1899 when thousands of stampeders pursued a way over the pass in search of Yukon gold. Huge tent cities mushroomed on the trail, and hundreds of horses were sent to their deaths—little evidence of this remains today. Most small, moveable mementos have been illegally removed by latter-day pilgrims, so there is little left of the trail of artifacts seen just a few years ago. Only large objects, such as sledge runners, boat skeletons, telegraph cables, and a derelict cable housing, which stands like a scarecrow against the sky under the pass, remain as mute testimony to those frantic years.

The route of the stampeders, from salt water at Skagway through the coastal mountains to the Canadian interior, is one of unsurpassed beauty. The broad flat-bottomed Dyea Valley at the beginning of the trail narrows into a steep-sided V-shaped valley of hanging glaciers, wild mountain streams, and crenelated ridges.

Mountain goats are often seen at these higher elevations. On the north side of the pass open, lake-studded, gentler country descends into the boreal forests of the Canadian interior.

Most modern trekkers start from Dyea, because this is the direction of the stampede, and from here the history follows a logical progression. Some 1,500 to 2,000 people now traverse the trail during the short summer months. Plan this trip well in advance, and take the following information into consideration.

***Customs clearance:*** Customs clearance must be obtained before starting. Those going northbound should call Canadian Customs at

*Stampeders in the gorge above Canyon City, Chilkoot Trail. (Photo courtesy Alaska State Library)*

Fraser (403-821-4111) or Whitehorse (403-667-6471). Those going south should call U.S. Customs in Skagway (907-983-2325). There is no phone in Dyea, so make the call before leaving Skagway.

*Trail administration:* The Chilkoot Trail is part of the Klondike Gold Rush Historical Park and is administered jointly by the U.S. National Park Service and Parks Canada. Prospective hikers should visit the NPS Visitor Center in Skagway to learn of current trail conditions. The summer ranger and warden stations are manned between June and September, and active flagging is done on the trail during that time.

*Access:* The trailhead can be reached by taxi from Skagway. Those with their own car should leave it at the ranger station in Dyea. Those walking from town may take the footbridge off First Avenue (see S5 Yakutania Point) as a shortcut, lessening the overall distance to about 7 miles.

On the northern end, between May and late September, a White Pass and Yukon Route (WP&YR) rail vehicle will pick up people in Bennett and take them to Log Cabin, Fraser, or Skagway. Passengers are advised to book passage in advance. Hikers are not authorized to walk the railroad tracks when the trains are running, but the Canadian NPS is working on a new trail between Lake Lindeman and the Klondike Highway at Log Cabin. A regular summer bus service runs between Skagway and Whitehorse with stops at Fraser and Carcross. Travelers can also make prior arrangements with Chilkoot Boat Tours for boat pickup from Bennett to Carcross. (See appendix C for phones and addresses.)

**Precautions:** A hiker should be in good physical shape and have struck a lasting partnership with his boots. A tent with rainfly, cooking stove, at least one day of extra food and fuel, warm, windproof and waterproof clothing (including hat and gloves), sunglasses, sleeping bag, and the Ten Essentials (see "Safety" in the Introduction) should be carried. Also take along identification and money.

Storms generally generate south of the divide and spill over the pass into Canadian territory. Weather conditions can be dramatically different from one side to the other any time of the year. Expect fog, cold, snow, and high winds on top. In summer, the trail is flagged, but it can still be lost in poor visibility. In winter, as much as 3 feet of snow can fall on the pass overnight, and up to 20 feet can accumulate here during a season.

In winter, temperatures can be extreme on and north of the pass, as low as −50 degrees Fahrenheit, and the wind chill factor (a little over 1 degree Fahrenheit for every mile per hour wind speed) should be considered.

Avalanche danger exists from March to May above Sheep Camp, and until early July north of the pass. Check with rangers or park headquarters (at the visitor center) if in doubt.

Follow the marked trail when traveling over spring and summer snows. Beware of rotten snow bridges and of deep holes when stepping off boulders onto snowfields. For the same reason, stay away from snow edges above swift-flowing streams, and do not be tempted to slide down snow slopes when the base cannot be seen.

Be careful not to dislodge rocks on the steep talus slopes, because of the possibility of hitting someone below. Large parties should stay together to lessen the chance of stragglers being hit.

At the height of the summer, when foot traffic is heavy, bear encounters are unlikely, though not inconceivable. Sightings of big game, such as moose and black bears on the Canadian side, and brown and black bears on the United States side, are more likely in spring and fall. Grizzly sightings on the Canadian side are rare. Bears fish the Taiya River below Canyon City, and black bears have been a problem to hikers near Dan Johnson Lake, Bare Loon Lake, and in Dyea Valley. Always

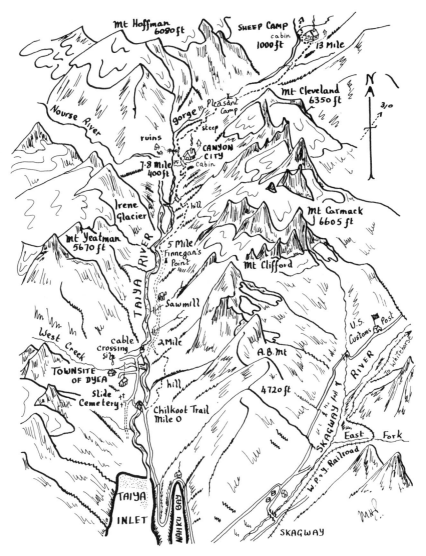

keep a clean camp, and cook away from tents. Guns are not allowed on the trail.

Topographic maps should be taken. For country north of the Chilkoot Pass (104M series), apply to the Department of Indian Affairs and Northern Development in Whitehorse (see appendix C). Travelers are advised to obtain maps beforehand, although it is possible they will be available in Skagway.

*Alaska Centennial Memorial, Chilkoot Pass*

***Regulations and recommendations:*** Except in emergency, hikers may camp only in designated sites where toilet facilities are available. The cabins at Canyon City, Sheep Camp, and Lindeman City are for day use only, for all comers. Tent camping is allowed at these sites; also at Finnegan's Point, Pleasant Camp, Happy Camp, Deep Lake, Dan Johnson Lake, Bare Loon Lake, and Bennett. The two shelters on the Canadian side directly below the pass at the south end of Crater Lake are for emergency use only.

Fires are not allowed in the Canadian park, except in Lindeman, where firewood is provided for the cabin stoves. Because of the numbers of people hiking the area, firewood is scarce. Plan to do without fires except in emergency. Also, help keep the lakes and streams free from contamination. Take a canvas or plastic bucket along to wash in to avoid direct contact with pristine water courses. The NPS recommends that all drinking water be boiled for one minute. (See "Giardiasis" under "Safety" in the Introduction.)

Do not disturb artifacts.

For help, summer ranger stations are located in Dyea, Sheep Camp, and a warden station at Lindeman City. Skagway has a year-round office. Bulletin boards for current trail conditions and messages are placed at Lindeman City and Log Cabin.

*Strategy:* Inexperienced hikers should take two days to reach Sheep Camp, stopping over at Canyon City (which is worth the extra time). Also trekkers are encouraged to wait out any bad weather at Sheep Camp and save the Chilkoot Pass for the next day. It is often hard to tell, so be prepared to return if the weather deteriorates after starting the final climb to the Scales.

For an interesting day or overnight trip when the WP&YR is shut down, drive to Log Cabin (see map). Park the car, then walk or ski (depending on how advanced winter is) to Bennett using a combination of railroad and trail. The round-trip distance is about 18 miles, but the going is easy, elevation loss minimal, and it can be walked or skiied in less than 10 hours.

# DYEA TO SHEEP CAMP

**TIME:** 6–7 hours
**DISTANCE:** 13 miles
**ELEVATION GAIN:** 1,700 feet

Those driving to the trailhead should take the highway north out of Skagway for 2 miles and turn left at the first road beyond the bridge, signposted Dyea. Park at the campground and ranger station, 8 miles from town. Half a mile beyond the campground, immediately before the Taiya River crossing, look for the Chilkoot Trail sign on the right side of the road. Those walking to Dyea may use the footbridge across the Skagway River at the south end of town as a shortcut. Turn left, then right up a dirt track that meets the Dyea road at the top of a steep hill (see also S5 Yakutania Point).

Almost immediately, the trail climbs steeply about 300 feet, then drops back to the Taiya River to join an old wagon road used in the 1950s for logging. This is followed past a ruined sawmill (3 miles) to Finnegan's Point, formerly a toll bridge and roadhouse and now a designated campsite. High above, frozen in mid-flight, is the Irene Glacier.

A well-defined footpath follows the river, then climbs over a couple of hills before dropping back to the river where it crosses a side creek. Here, a brief open area gives views of Mount Cleveland and the valley. The trail climbs, then drops about 100 feet to Canyon City (7.8 miles). The shelter contains some interesting historical reading, which is worth a few minutes before hurrying on. The old Canyon City site can be found across a suspension bridge, about 0.5 mile north of the shelter and campground. It makes a pleasant diversion, and a few large items of historical interest are left, such as a boiler, a stove, some sled runners, and some scattered cans.

Shortly after Canyon City, the route climbs steeply above a gorge. In the winter of 1898, stampeders climbed the frozen riverbed, but now the path stays well above the river, and to the west, it opens to lovely views of ice fields and the Sawtooth ridge above the Nourse River. High glaciers spill off Mount Hoffman above the gorge, and there are glimpses of the river far below. The trail descends about 300 feet to Pleasant Camp, approximately 800 feet elevation, and 10.5 miles from the start. (Those descending toward Dyea should take note of these hills. They are killers to tired hikers who think the end is in sight.)

Pleasant Camp is in tall trees by the Taiya River, with open views up the valley. It is the only camp on this side with no side streams; water has to be taken from the main river, which is turbid and possibly contaminated. About a mile above Pleasant Camp, cross a beautiful, but expensive-looking suspension bridge over a swift, glacial side creek fed by Mount Cleveland snowfields. A ranger station is passed close to Sheep Camp, elevation 1,000 feet. Allow 3 to 4 hours from Canyon City.

# SHEEP CAMP TO DEEP LAKE

**TIME:** 8 hours or overnight
**DISTANCE:** 10 miles
**ELEVATION GAIN:** 3,000 feet

The footpath, running northeast, climbs steadily as the valley gets narrower. Once above the alder and onto rock, the path is more difficult to follow; when boulder hopping, keep a sharp lookout for cairns and marker ribbons. Stay on the right bank of the stream until above the ruins of an old tramway building, then cross the stream and follow large stone cairns to reach the Scales, almost at the head of the valley. If snow obliterates the trail, follow the current markers, which are checked periodically by park rangers. Be wary of footsteps that lead away from the marked trail; rotten snow can conceal deep holes.

From the Scales (2,620 feet), the path goes in a north-northeasterly direction to Chilkoot Pass and the U.S.-Canadian border (3,535 feet). The climb is steep, up loose rock, scree, and snow. Be careful not to dislodge rocks onto climbers below. Pass an Alaskan commemorative marker about 200 yards south of the summit, and from here the views are superb. The deep cleft of the valley is many shades of blue, as it wends its way below snow-carpeted, shaggy peaks towards the sea. Keep an eye out for mountain goats; they may be seen

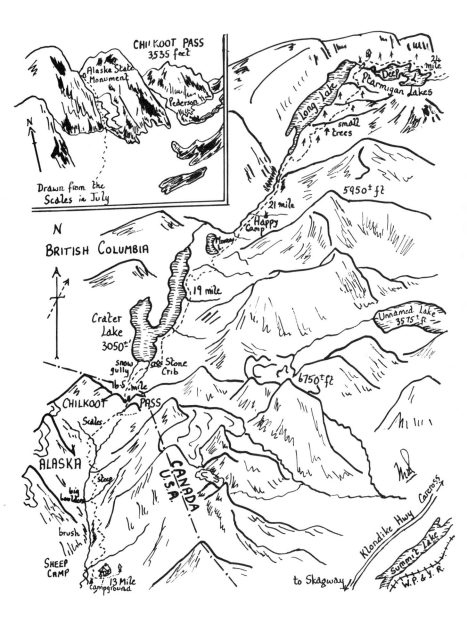

*Boot Hill, Lindeman Lake*

in and around the pass. Allow 5 to 6 hours from Sheep Camp to the summit.

Storms roar through the Chilkoot Pass as a matter of principle every day or so, and the summit is exposed to the unmitigated fury of a southwesterly blow. Anyone caught in a storm is advised to seek shelter directly over the summit, or if possible, find the two emergency shelters at the Stone Crib above Crater Lake (3,210 feet elevation). Travelers are permitted to stop briefly at the shelters for food and drink, and to change clothes, but then must move on. No overnight camping is allowed. A stove is essential for making hot drinks; water is plentiful north of the summit. Travelers are warned the shelters tend to be crowded during bad weather.

The Stone Crib, a disintegrated cable housing for the old tramway, is about 0.5 mile northeast and 300 feet below the summit on the

Canadian side of the divide. A snow slope descends from the summit to Crater Lake; traverse to the right about 150 feet above the lake. Be sure to pick up the trail running along the south end of Crater Lake to the Stone Crib. If caught in early summer fog, proceed carefully down the snow slope, because it sometimes ends as a sheer dropoff over deep water.

The path, marked with cairns or snow wands, follows the east shore of Crater Lake in a treeless country liberally sprinkled with lakes and streams—often wet underfoot. Then it gradually descends past a small tarn, Morrow Lake, into a shallow river valley and sparse, stunted, hill-hugging trees. Happy Camp sits on a side hill, 7.5 miles from Sheep Camp.

Below Happy Camp the route follows the river through a small gorge, then ascends about 450 feet above Long Lake to avoid its rocky east shore. The trail drops to a wooden bridge spanning the boiling white and green cataract connecting Long Lake with Deep Lake. Camping is allowed on the hill to the west of the bridge. Elevation of the lakes is about 2,850 feet. Here the scenery has softened considerably from the wild, open country of the pass and the somber black crags above the Scales. The trees are taller, though still sparse, and the lakes provide an idyllic setting for camping. There are extensive views of the mountains above Tutshi Lake, on the far side of the Klondike Highway.

# DEEP LAKE TO BENNETT

**TIME:** 6 hours or overnight
**DISTANCE:** 10 miles
**ELEVATION GAIN:** 500 feet

The route skirts the north shore of Deep Lake, to its outflow, then it drops gradually 700 feet to Lake Lindeman, above the river gorge. At the east end of Deep Lake, watch for sledges and runners left behind by the 1898 Gold Rush. The wooded slopes are predominantly alpine fir, with lodgepole pine mixed in. About halfway down the gorge, off the trail to the right, is a distant view of Lake Lindeman and a mountain range south of Tutshi Lake that should not be missed. Almost at the end of the long downhill, after rounding a corner, the southern shore of Lake Lindeman lies at one's feet.

Lindeman City (26 trail miles from Dyea), 5.5 miles from Happy Camp and 7 miles from Bennett, has two cabins and a warden station. The "WCI Engineers" built the upper (west) cabin in 1968 and the lower cabin, about 400 yards east with views down the lake, in 1971.

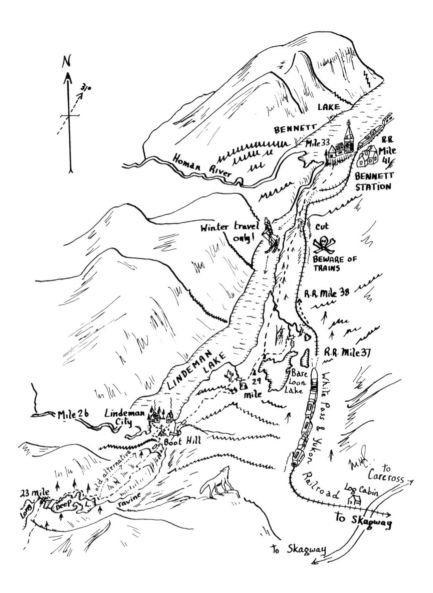

N
3|°

Homan River

LAKE
BENNETT
Mile 33

R.R. Mile 41
BENNETT STATION

Winter travel only!

cut

BEWARE OF TRAINS

R.R. Mile 38

R.R. Mile 37

LINDEMAN LAKE

Mile 26

Lindeman City

29 mile

Bare Loon Lake

White Pass & Yukon Railroad

Boot Hill

old alternative

ravine

23 mile

Deep L.

to Carcross

Log Cabin

To Skagway

to Skagway

A trail register may be found in one or both. Both cabins are available for day use only to all comers. The stoves are adequate for cooking, but firewood is limited, and the indiscriminate cutting of wood is discouraged. A bare twenty years ago, trees around Lake Lindeman were scarce, because they had been decimated by the Klondike stampeders in their haste to make boats for the long trip downriver. Now, at this altitude, lodgepole pine has the ascendency.

The Canadian warden station is located approximately 400 yards from the cemetery, on the trail to the lower cabin. Hikers are requested to register with the warden, and all bear sightings should be reported. Boot Hill, the burial ground for the souls who did not make it to Dawson, is situated on the main trail to Bennett, and it offers good views of the lake and encircling mountains.

From the upper cabin, follow the most southerly trail under Boot Hill and cross Moose Creek. After the bridge, the path climbs about 200 feet; look behind for good views of the lake and campgrounds. Two miles of beautiful, undulating trail brings hikers through pine forests to Dan Johnson Lake, and shortly afterwards (0.5 mile) to Bare Loon Lake. Close to the latter campsite, the trail divides. The right fork goes to the railroad tracks, about 20 minutes away. It is the quickest route out to the Klondike Highway when the trains are not running. Turn right at the tracks, and Log Cabin is 5 gentle miles uphill (a 500-foot elevation gain). Hikers are reminded they are not authorized to walk the railroad tracks when trains are running.

The left fork follows the lake fairly closely to Bennett, allowing views southwest up Lindeman Lake, and toward the pass. Watch for an old gravesite about 1 mile from Bennett; soft sand is encountered for that last mile.

Bennett Church overlooks the lake at the end of the trail, and the WP&YR station is about 100 yards east of the church. When the station is shut down there are no facilities in Bennett. Below the church, to the west, there is a camping area and outhouse by the 1-mile rapids connecting Lindeman Lake with Lake Bennett.

## S2
# LOWER DEWEY LAKE

**TIME:** 20 minutes
**DISTANCE:** 0.7 mile
**ELEVATION GAIN:** 500 feet
**RATING:** easy
**TYPE:** pleasant wooded bench, fishing, swimming in summer; skating
    in winter
**MAP:** Skagway B-1, 1 inch:1 mile

On the east edge of town, a trail system administered by the city climbs to the first bench, 500 feet above sea level. It offers interest to young and old, the casual and serious walker. The first 0.5 mile to the reservoir is steep in places, and during March or April, ice may necessitate crampons or creepers. Also, during spring, take a hat along as protection against nesting goshawks. The trail complex is administered by the city of Skagway, and it is within walking distance of town.

The absence of large evergreen trees on both the north and south ends of the bench is due to a devastating fire in 1912. Mushrooms are plentiful on the bench from late July to September, and edible mushrooms such as *Lactarius deliciosus* (orange delicious), Russula, and Boletus may be found. Make a positive identification and pick at your own risk! Two toilets are placed in strategic positions along the trail (see map).

From the ferry, walk into town to the NPS visitor center. Turn right, then left up a dirt road by the railroad tracks for two short blocks. A broad gravel pathway travels uphill to the right on the hill side of the tracks. After crossing a stream and waterlines, the route goes 120 yards up the hill to a large flat rock and a view of town. Forty feet above this point, the trail divides. The larger one to the right is the shortest route to the reservoir and Lower Dewey Lake. The one to the left is the shortest route to Icy Lake and Upper Reid Falls, and it connects with the long trail that traverses the north bench from Lower Dewey Lake.

About 30 yards below the reservoir, turn right along a broad footpath to a trail division 200 yards farther along. (A parallel path girds the reservoir.) Turn left for the north shore of Lower Dewey Lake, about 160 yards away, and North Bench.

Turn right for the west shore of Lower Dewey Lake, about 200

*South end of Lower Dewey Lake*

yards distant. This trail runs southward along the west shore of the lake, another 0.5 mile (1.5 miles from town). It continues as a primitive pathway to Sturgill's Landing (see S4 Magic Forest). Another primitive route follows the eastern shoreline of Lower Dewey Lake, across an old spillway and along some rusty, overgrown tracks that belonged to a stone quarry in the vicinity. This route joins the major trail system about 100 yards north of the lake. The shortest way back to town goes left to the lake, then right to the original trail division. From here turn right for town. (A smaller pathway follows the reservoir shore parallel to, and to the right of, the main route.) If in doubt refer to the map! The circle route of Lower Dewey Lake back to town is 2.7 miles.

# NORTHERN BENCH

**TIME:** 30 minutes
**DISTANCE:** 1 mile to town
**ELEVATION GAIN:** 200 ± feet

From the northwest corner of Lower Dewey Lake, go north across a small bridge and walk between two streams. The trail round the east shore of Lower Dewey Lake turns off to the right. Shortly after crossing a large stream (300 yards from the lake), the trail to Upper Dewey Lake splits off to the right. Close by is a toilet. The main path along the north bench climbs gently, crosses another stream by a wood camp, and takes a sharp right into goshawk territory. A disused logging road goes straight ahead, leading nowhere in particular. Stay on the trail to a major intersection, about 15 minutes from Lower Dewey Lake (or half a mile north). Turn left for Skagway (half a mile) or continue north to Icy Lake (1 mile distant) and Upper Reid Falls, 850 feet elevation (almost 2 miles).

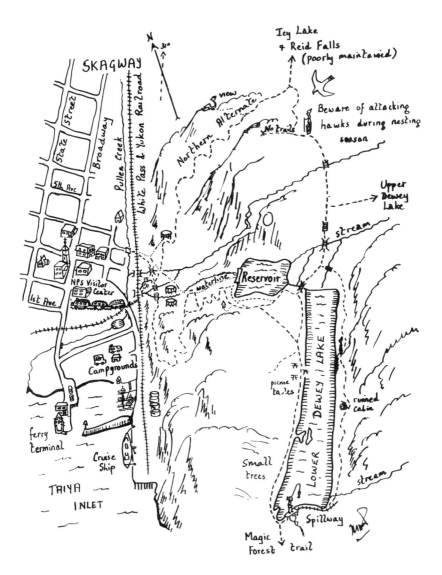

The descent to Skagway is gentler than the direct trail to the reservoir. A good viewpoint of the town, ferry, and cruise ships is located about 150 yards below the intersection, off the path to the right. Be very careful near the edge. Another viewpoint is located on the far side of a large watertower, close to the end of trail. This route is useful as an alternative onto the bench when the main trail is icy.

## S3
# UPPER DEWEY LAKE

**TIME:** 3 hours to cabin
**DISTANCE:** 3.0 miles from town
**ELEVATION GAIN:** to cabin, 3,080 feet
**RATING:** strenuous
**ACCESS:** via S2 Lower Dewey Lake
**TYPE:** forest, alpine flora and fauna
**MAP:** Skagway B-1, 1 inch:1 mile
Overnight cabin; take a cooking stove

To enjoy vistas of upper Taiya Inlet and the surrounding mountains, a hike to Upper Dewey Lake is a must. A primitive cabin sits by the lake, at 3,000 feet above sea level. Breakfast can be supplemented with rainbow and eastern brook trout by those who take a fishing pole and a license. People staying overnight should take a cooking stove, and please remember that wood is scarce. Do not chop down any living trees. Leave the cabin clean for those who follow. This area is administered by the city of Skagway.

The route to Upper Dewey Lake is reached by walking to Lower Dewey Lake (see S2 Lower Dewey Lake) and turning left along the north bench trail. The Upper Dewey Lake junction is on the right, 0.8 mile from town. It climbs steeply at first through a series of switchbacks, and at 800 feet above the bench, there is a view of town and the reservoir. Farther up, the climb eases, and the route follows Dewey Creek closely for a short way. It finally emerges from the trees into a muskeg meadow, where there are views of Mount Harding and the inlet below. Note the point of re-entry for the return in case of fog. Cross the meadow (almost due east) toward the great mountain cirque to reach the lake. The cabin is on the right, on the far side of the spillway.

*Taiya Inlet from the bench above Upper Dewey Lake*

For those staying overnight in good weather, a walk north to the 4,100-foot bench for views of Twin Dewey Peaks, surrounding mountains and valleys, or southward to the Devils Punchbowl, is worth the extra time. There is no trail going north, but hiking is fairly easy if care is taken and hiking boots are worn. Take lunch, warm clothing, map, and compass.

## DEVILS PUNCHBOWL

**TIME:** 1 ± hour from cabin
**DISTANCE:** 1.2 miles
**ELEVATION GAIN:** 620 ± feet

From the cabin there is a small footpath leading south up the alpine bench to an overlook of Punchbowl Lake. Once out of the trees, the ground is lichen covered, and a mile above the cabin, the view is stunning. Skagway is a "toy town," almost 4,000 feet below with toy cruise ships and ferries, and toy airplanes taking off and landing at the tiny airstrip. The entire upper Taiya Inlet is surrounded by a sweep of mountains, most unnamed and unclimbed. About 250 yards farther south, and 100 feet below, is the clear, green, but cold waters of Punchbowl Lake. Camping is not recommended here, because the ground is rough underfoot, and the lake is not ice free until late summer.

Some energetic souls climb up the shaley, steep slope behind the overlook to the end of ridge, about 5,000 feet elevation. The slope is steep and loose, but the view from the top is magnificent. A register is kept in a jar on the "summit."

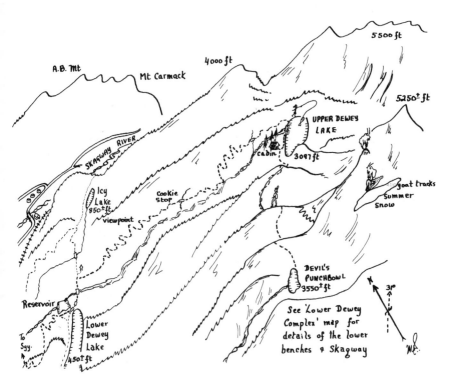

# S4
# MAGIC FOREST

**TIME:** 2 hours
**DISTANCE:** 3.2 miles from Skagway
**ELEVATION GAIN:** 1,000 feet round trip
**RATING:** moderate
**ACCESS:** through S2 Lower Dewey Lake; small boat
**TYPE:** forest, beach
**MAP:** Skagway B-1, 1 inch:1 mile
Exposed anchorage at Sturgill's landing
Beach campsite

Many years ago Barbara Kalen, a local trail enthusiast, named the trail to Sturgill's Landing "Magic Forest," because these woods have an aura about them. In two groves south of Dewey Lake, the trees are straight and tall, the forest floor is moss covered, and sunlight streams through the trees rather like the light in an ancient cathedral. Between the large groves, a logged patch has grown back with pine, birch, and hemlock. Also, a rusty winch and cable, where logs were rolled to tide level in 1920, remain alongside the trail about halfway down to the beach. The route ends on the shoreline of Taiya Inlet. There is a picnic spot and campsite complete with toilets and garbage pit. Hikers could walk there with camping gear, stay overnight, then be picked up by boat the next morning or late evening when the winds are calm; or be put ashore in the early morning and walk out the same day. Boaters beware: the anchorage at Sturgill's Landing is poor and is exposed to northerly and southerly blows.

From Skagway, walk to the south end of Lower Dewey Lake (S2), 1.4 miles. The path becomes less well defined and divides. The left fork continues around the shoreline; the right fork goes through the Magic Forest to Sturgill's Landing. The trail descends almost immediately and may be somewhat brushy at first through the old burn area of 1912, but soon it reaches big trees and pleasant walking. Keep an eye out for sudden turns in this section of trail. About halfway—or little over 1 mile—the winch should be seen in an opening of trees with views across the inlet.

Shortly afterward the trail skirts a small muskeg pool, and with another sharp turn, runs back into the Magic Forest. Before too long the stream outflow from Lower Dewey Lake can be heard. The route turns right, but a pathway to the left descends to the stream. The trail then drops steeply above the stream gully towards the inlet. About 60 feet above the shore, look for a pathway to the right going toward picnic tables and toilets, which are visible through the trees. Do not try to go straight down.

This route is easier to follow now than it was in earlier years, but careless hikers can still get lost. Be sure to have map and compass, and if the days are short, carry a flashlight. Bear in mind that this route stays on a gently sloping bench, with Lower Dewey Lake to the north, the inlet to the west, and the stream outflow to the east. The beach campgrounds are administered by the USFS.

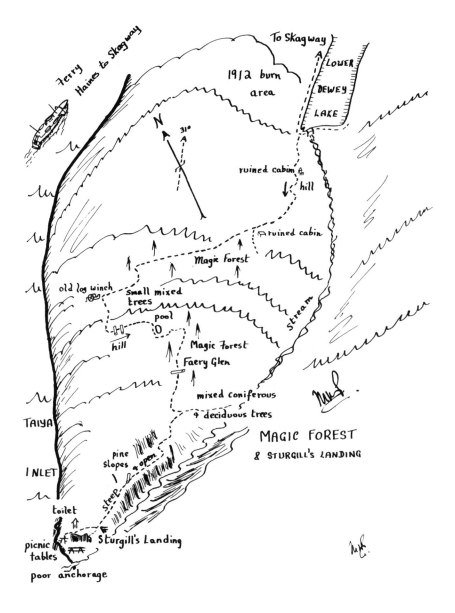

Ferry Haines to Skagway

To Skagway

LOWER DEWEY LAKE

1912 burn area

N    31°

ruined cabin    hill

ruined cabin

Magic Forest

old log winch

Small mixed trees

hill

pool

Magic Forest Faery Glen

stream

mixed coniferous & deciduous trees

TAIYA

MAGIC FOREST & STURGILL'S LANDING

INLET

pine slopes & open

steep

toilet

picnic tables

Sturgill's Landing

poor anchorage

# S5
# YAKUTANIA POINT

**TIME:** 15–20 minutes
**DISTANCE:** 1 mile
**ELEVATION GAIN:** insignificant
**RATING:** easy
**TYPE:** shoreline, picnic, exercise grounds

A footbridge on the west end of town crosses the Skagway River, giving access to a picnic site on the shore of Smugglers Cove and to milepost 4 on the Dyea Road. Physical fitness stations for limbering and general aerobics have been set up in the first 300 yards or so. The picnic site has a covered area, tables, and toilets, sheltered from prevailing winds in a pine grove below the shoreline rocks. It is a pleasant place to sit and observe sea mammals, pelagic ducks and gulls, and the sea traffic coming in and going out of Skagway. Smugglers Cove is an-

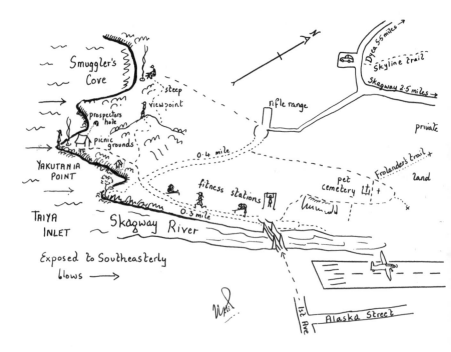

other 0.25 mile around the point and is also a favorite picnic site. This route affords a shortcut to milepost 4 on the Dyea Road and to the Skyline Trail.

Walk along First Avenue toward the river, skirting the south end of the airstrip. Stay off the strip. Cross the footbridge, and at the far side, turn left. After the last exercise station, turn right up a steep dirt road to reach the Dyea Road, or go straight along a narrow footpath to get to Yakutania Point. A right fork in the trees climbs 150 feet above sea level to a view of Taiya Inlet. It traverses the hillside and drops steeply to Smugglers Cove. Here there is a small shingle beach and open meadow.

The trails to the right of the footbridge are steep and rough, but they will bring the wanderer to a view of the river and a pet cemetery (see map). One can wander back across the hillside to the upper dirt road. The walk and picnic areas are administered by the city of Skagway.

---

## S6
# GOLD RUSH CEMETERY

**TIME:** 40 minutes from town
**DISTANCE:** 4.8 miles from Skagway via S5 Yakutania Point
**ELEVATION GAIN:** none
**RATING:** easy
**TYPE:** historical, waterfall

This makes a pleasant evening or morning stroll from tour ship or ferry, through town, to the site where Jefferson Randolph (Soapy) Smith and Frank Reid lie buried. Soapy was a gambler and con man, and Reid, a city engineer, was the town hero who dispatched Soapy in a duel, July 8, 1898. An explanatory pamphlet is available at the visitor center. Behind the graveyard a short trail of about 50 yards goes to the base of the waterfall named after Reid. These falls, which have a drop of about 300 feet, are especially attractive in winter when they become almost totally frozen over.

From the ferry terminal, walk into town along Broadway (the historical district). Turn left up one of the side streets, then right up State Street, and continue north until the road makes a left turn to cross the

Skagway River. Keep going straight, and follow the railroad along a dirt road, across some shunting lines. After a little more than 0.25 mile, cross the tracks. Reach the cemetery about 300 yards farther on. People with cars should turn left towards the river, then right on the far side of the marshalling yards.

Do not attempt to scramble on the cliffs above the falls; the rock is loose and crumbly and not worth the risk. Always beware of trains when crossing the tracks. Bring ice creepers during March and April for the short path to the falls, as the waterfall is highly photogenic, and the path often slippery at this time of year. The Gold Rush cemetery is administered by the city of Skagway.

*Gold Rush cemetery*

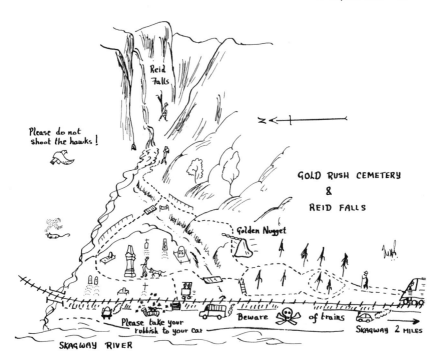

---

## S7

# SKYLINE TRAIL AND A. B. MOUNTAIN

**TIME:** 3.5 hours to 3,500-foot summit

**DISTANCE:** 3.3 miles to view summit (4.8 miles from Skagway via S5 Yakutania Point)

**ELEVATION GAIN:** 3,500 ± feet

**RATING:** strenuous

**TYPE:** pine and fir forests, open mountain

**MAPS:** Skagway B-1 and C-1, 1 inch:1 mile

A. B. Mountain, the peak on the west side of the Skagway Valley, dominates the town from this angle. The Skyline Trail, which gives access to the lower ridge, is particularly rich in moss and lichen-covered

rocks and has fairly open, mixed deciduous, pine, hemlock, and fir forests. The trail continues up the mountain, where sweeping views of the inlet, Taiya Valley, and surrounding sharp, glacier-hung peaks are revealed. One can be satisfied with an hour (a couple from town) through the woods, or spend an entire day on the mountain. An especially attractive time is late September or early October when birches, willows, and cottonwoods turn a brilliant gold. On sunny days the woods are radiant. Do not venture above treeline without foul-weather gear, and the Ten Essentials.

The Skyline trailhead is 1.5 walking miles from town. Cross the footbridge over the Skagway River (see S4 Magic Forest) at the south end of town, turn left up the dirt road, then right up a steep hill to the Dyea Road. Turn left, and a few yards along the road, at the highest point of the hill, the trail should be seen on the right. If driving to the trailhead, go north 2 miles out of Skagway and turn left onto the Dyea Road. The trail starts close to milepost 4 on the north side of the road. A small parking area (large enough for two or three cars) is on the left. The path goes over a bank by a derelict building, through mixed birch and willow woods, and over small rock bluffs. After about 20 or 30 minutes of steady climbing, a large rock is passed, about 20 paces off the trail to the right. From here some of the best views of Skagway and Taiya Inlet are obtained. The main route climbs steadily until crossing a stream 1.5 miles from the road. Here the path enters mixed hemlock and alpine fir forests. The base of A. B. Mountain is reached 0.5 to 0.75 mile from the stream crossing. A stream is again crossed, and the route climbs steeply through alder and devil's club, crosses the stream once more (now a trickle) and stays on the right (east) side of a gully.

As soon as the slope eases off and the gully can be crossed, cross over it. Ignore the path that continues to climb; it goes into an almost impenetrable thicket of mountain hemlock. Keep a sharp lookout for trail markers—cairns and ribbon—and build up the existing cairns, as many people get lost here. At the far side of the gully, look back at the route, so it can be recognized on the return. Then continue uphill toward the northwest over alpine meadows to the ridge. The views are panoramic. Skagway is laid out like a map, and the blue waters of Taiya Inlet recede beneath a wall of graceful, snow-covered peaks.

The ridge may be climbed as far as is desired, with expanding views up West Creek, across Dewey Peaks, and to the Sawtooth Range above the Skagway River. The last peak visible from Skagway is about

*Skagway from A. B. Mountain*

3,500 feet above sea level, and the ridge from here to A. B. Mountain, 5,000 ± feet, is about 2 miles. It is gentle, broad, and little traveled. Wildlife, such as mountain goats and more rarely bears, may be seen on the ridge.

If visibility deteriorates when descending, spend extra time to find the cairns. Do not attempt to come off the mountain any other way.

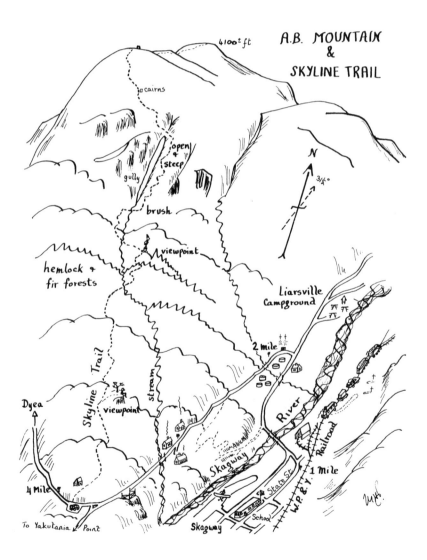

# S8
# DENVER GLACIER

**TIME:** 4–5 hours from town
**DISTANCE:** 3.5 miles; 7 miles from Gold Rush cemetery
**ELEVATION GAIN:** 1,200 feet
**RATING:** difficult because condition is poor
**ACCESS:** WP&YR flag stop May to Sept.
**TYPE:** deep valley, glacial river, forest
**MAPS:** Skagway B-1 and C-1; 1 inch:1 mile
Avalanche danger

This walk takes hikers under the mighty walls of the Sawtooth Range (5,000 to 7,000 feet elevation), and it ends in the brush of the Denver Glacier moraine on the east side of Twin Dewey Peaks, which dominate the valley. Unfortunately, what little maintenance is done on the trail is done by local residents. The glacier has receded about 1,000 feet up the mountain since the 1940s, and thick brush has reasserted itself on the moraine. Thus, it is unlikely many hikers will get too close, but if the glacier is reached, beware of falling ice. Chances of seeing wildlife in the area are good, except during hunting season. Make plenty of noise when in brush because of the likelihood of encountering bears.

This USFS trail starts a few yards short of milepost 6 on the WP&YR, 3.5 miles from the Gold Rush cemetery (S6). Turn right a few yards before the tracks cross the East Fork Skagway River and follow the river's south bank upstream. The path plunges into spruce and hemlock forests then emerges on the bank of the swiftly flowing, glacial stream. Here there are good views of the Sawtooth spires on the north side of the valley. It then climbs a steep hill and traverses a slide area now covered with alder and devil's club. After about 2 miles, the trail leaves the East Fork Skagway River and turns south up the glacial outwash of the Denver Glacier. It crosses two small streams in devil's club grottos, then opens onto a rock platform above a miniature gorge—a good lunch stop. In the past, a bridge straddled the stream here to give access to a partially ruined hunter's cabin on the far side and to the "S" Glacier, 3 miles up the main valley.

The route continues south, but the quality deteriorates even further. While nebulous at first, it is possible to find, except at a couple of

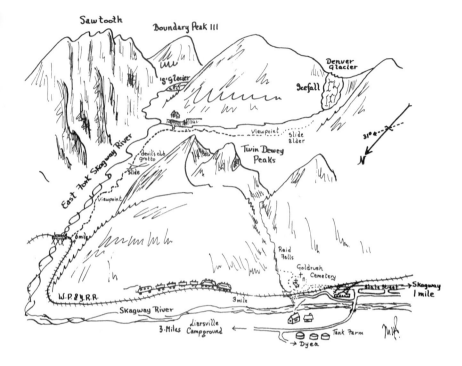

slide areas. The route then gets lost in thick brush. The moraine is about 1 mile farther on.

Winter is a good time to explore the valley on snowshoes or skis, because rivers are easier to cross and the brush is buried in deep snow. In spring avalanche danger is high; avoid the valley in March and April.

# S9
# LAUGHTON GLACIER

**TIME:** 40 minutes along trail; overnight stay recommended
**DISTANCE:** 1.5 miles
**ELEVATION GAIN:** 200 feet; from town 2,100 feet
**RATING:** easy
**ACCESS:** by WP&YR to Glacier Station (milepost 14)
**TYPE:** forest, mountain cirque, cascading glacier
**MAPS:** Skagway C-1, 1 inch:1 mile, or Canadian Sheet: White Pass 104
    M/11 East, 1.25 inch:1 mile
Overnight cabin

Laughton Glacier Trail gives access to a cirque of immense hanging glaciers that adhere to the 3,000-foot walls of the Sawtooth Range. It is one of the few places where wild mountain scenery is accessible to those who do not have the trappings of the technical mountaineer. If a stay in the cabin is planned, arrangements should be made with the

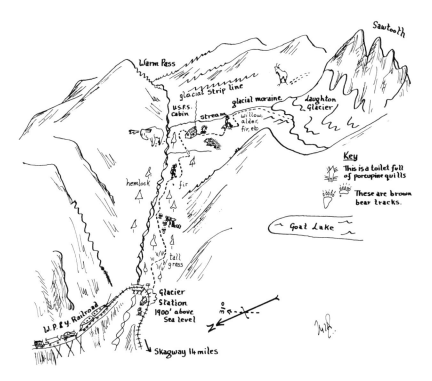

*Laughton Glacier (Photo by Barbara D. Kalen)*

USFS in Juneau, or at the NPS visitor center on Second and Broadway in Skagway. Two excursion trains from Skagway run to White Pass daily, so a day hike in and out is possible. Check with the WP&YR offices in town for times, because they vary depending on the cruise ship schedules.

The trail starts on the south side of the Skagway River bridge, at Glacier Station, 11.5 miles from the Gold Rush cemetery. Travelers are warned not to walk the tracks, because there is no room for foot passage and trains simultaneously on trestles or along certain sections of line. Avalanche and rockfall danger, especially on the upper levels of track, is extreme.

The route follows the south bank of the river upstream toward Warm Pass. It passes almost immediately into a tall grass meadow, then enters forest. River and trail continue in close proximity, and meet at a point where the river narrows and runs through a rock cleft. Some of the small streams that are crossed have slippery logs as bridges; also windfalls cause occasional interruptions in what is otherwise smooth traveling.

The Forest Service cabin sits in a strategic spot, about 1,000 feet below and 1 mile distant from the glacier, at the confluence of the Laughton Glacier outwash and the Skagway River. An overnight stop is highly recommended. The cabin has an ax, cooking utensils, and sleeping space for six people. The stove is adequate for cooking but it does not give off sufficient heat in the winter. Be sure to replace any wood used; do not cut living trees. Keep the camp clean. Make plenty of noise when going through brush, as encounters with bear or moose are possible. Goats may be seen high on the rock walls. Also note the trimline, or lower limit of trees, on the ridge opposite, showing the level of the glacier before recession occurred.

This USFS trail is recommended for both summer and winter travel. Do not venture on the glacier until snow bridges have melted, or unless skilled in glacier travel.

# S10
# LOST LAKE

**TIME FROM DYEA RANGER STATION:** 2 hours
**DISTANCE FROM RANGER STATION:** 2.9 miles
**ELEVATION GAIN:** 1,400 ± feet
**RATING:** moderate
**TYPE:** forest, hill, historical
**MAPS:** Skagway C-1, 1 inch:1 mile

A little-used and locally maintained trail climbs steeply to a small lake nestled in a fold of hill above the Dyea Valley. The lake offers swimming, a pleasant campsite, rainbow trout, and mosquitos. Instead

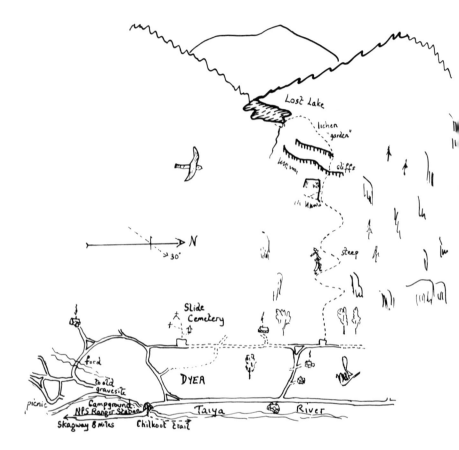

of flower gardens, this is a lichen paradise, *but they are fragile!* Please keep dogs in tow, and do not wander off the trail yourself into lichen areas.

Drive to Dyea and park at the NPS ranger station (or drive to the trailhead 1.4 miles farther along). Walk north along the road and take the third driveway on the left, 0.5 mile beyond the Taiya River bridge. Walk toward the hill westward, ignoring private driveways, and turn right at a T junction under the hillslope (0.3 mile from the road). Almost 180 yards on the left, there is an opening in the trees with limited parking off the narrow dirt road. (The NPS visitor center on Second and Broadway in Skagway has information on Dyea.)

Walk directly toward the hillslope on the path, and climb almost immediately up a series of steep banks, some of it as switchback. Follow tree blazes and signs of greatest tread. After about 50 minutes of steep climbing, the route appears to go across a large exposed rock. By all means go across for the view (keep small children back because of the danger of falling), but be sure to return to the original path and climb up the gully to its right. (Many people get lost here, ignore footmarks going directly up the rock and small paths at the top leading to the left—away from the correct route.) Continue over rock ledges deeply carpeted with mosses and lichens, although some have become threadbare through excessive trampling. Shortly after, the trail pauses on the lip of a huge rock overlooking Lost Lake, a black windless pool caught in a shallow bowl. It then drops steeply to the outflow.

# RETURN BY SLIDE CEMETERY

**TIME:** 1.5 hours from Lost Lake
**DISTANCE:** 3.4 miles
**ELEVATION GAIN:** none

Those going back to the ranger station in Dyea may decide to walk alongside the hill to Slide Cemetery. This is where most of the victims of the April 3, 1898 snowslide above Sheep Camp were buried. Also, the old wagon roads, against the hill on the west side of Dyea, make very pleasant walking.

When the trailhead is reached once more, turn right (south) along the dirt road and, instead of turning left at the T junction to return to the main road, keep going straight on. Do not attempt to drive this back road. Walk south ignoring side roads on both right and left, and the cemetery will be reached within 10 or 15 minutes (0.6 mile). To return to the main road, continue in the same direction to the next road junction 350 yards south. Turn left and walk for another 10 or 15 minutes. Turn right to cross the Taiya River once more.

# HAINES

HAINES is an incredibly beautiful place, with bristling, snow-covered peaks ringing the hamlet. It also has a lasting Native legacy. The valley was settled hundreds of years ago through a pass in the Chilkat Range, which gave native tribes in the interior access to the valley's rich fishery and wildlife habitat. Haines was called Dei Shu, or the "end of the trail." In 1897, Jack Dalton herded cattle from Haines to Dawson City to sell to stampeders. Now a road wends its way through the same pass to connect Haines with the Yukon and the "rest of the world." The southern access is the most scenic waterway in the world, the Inside Passage. Through it come the tourists and the groceries, by cruise ship, ferry, and barge.

The mountain's lower slopes are covered with a mixture of pine, spruce, hemlock, and willow. Cottonwoods reign in the river flats where bald eagles use the trees' crown for nesting and their branches as observation posts. As many as 3,000 resident and migrant birds congregate on the Council Grounds, an unfrozen stretch of river close to Klukwan, a Native village 21 miles up the Haines Highway. The best viewing time is November through December, when snow is on the ground, mists hang low over river and trees, and eagles can be seen in the hundreds at one glance. Their presence depends on a late run of salmon, which takes advantage of the open Chilkat River. This, in its turn, is caused by percolation of relatively warm ground water through the immense Tsirku alluvial fan.

A tent-only campsite is situated in Portage Cove on Beach Road, about 0.5 mile south of town. Also, two campgrounds, run by the state of Alaska for visitors with campers or tents, lie at road end north and south of town. One is by Chilkoot Lake beyond the head of Lutak Inlet; the other is in the Chilkat State Park close to tidewater with views of Rainbow and Davidson glaciers. Portage Cove is the jumping off place for the Battery Point and Mount Riley trails, and the Chilkat State Park has a tidewater walk to Seduction Point. Lutak has no hiking trail, but it is possible to bicycle along a logging road to the north end of Chilkoot Lake to a salmon spawning hole. Take a noisy bell along in case bears are present.

*Bald eagle*

# H1
# MOUNT RIPINSKY

**TIME:** 4 hours
**DISTANCE:** 4.5 miles
**ELEVATION GAIN:** 3,650 ± feet
**RATING:** strenuous
**TYPE:** forest, alpine
**MAPS:** Skagway A-2 and B-2

Mount Ripinsky dominates Haines to the northwest and has a register on its north peak. The summit offers expansive views of the town, tidal waters, a river estuary, and the jagged, glacier-hung peaks to the borders of Glacier Bay. An extended ridge walk over a 3,920-foot peak to Seven Mile Saddle on a clear day is hard to beat, although it is prob-

*Haines from Mount Ripinsky*

ably better going toward Haines for the constant views over the Lynn Canal. The trail was built and is maintained by the Haines Borough. The walk up is a steady climb through forests to alpine, but hikers should note that foul weather can bring fog, rain, and snow across the tops. The trail is easily lost in spring snows and on top during bad

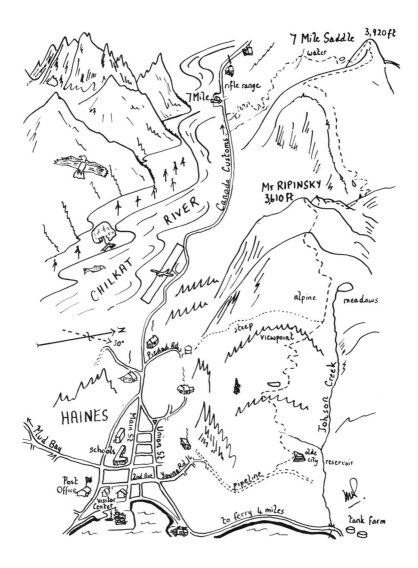

weather. When snows are gone (by mid-July), water is found where the trail meets Johnson Creek at 2,500 feet on Mount Ripinsky, a good camp site. A steep, primitive shortcut exists from Piedad Road, on the west end of town.

Walk north along Second Avenue toward Lutak and the ferry terminal. When the main road veers to the right, keep straight on up the hill, on Young Road. Go across and slightly right at the five-way junction; at all junctions choose the road that goes uphill, yet traverses the slope. Follow the rough, brushy road, an oil pipeline right-of-way, which parallels the inlet below (Lutak). After almost 1 mile of walking, the road dips downhill, and a tank farm can be seen in the distance. Here the Mount Ripinsky Trail starts to the left.

The path climbs gently past the old city water supply (not easily seen in brush close to the beginning) and through 1.5 miles of forest to a viewpoint at 1,700 feet. About 400 feet below Johnson Creek, or 0.2 mile farther along, the shortcut from Piedad Road joins the main trail. Here, the trees are small, and large open areas make camping desirable. The climb steepens, and the ridge offers magnificent views of the town. Please do not tread on the rare blue gentian at the best viewpoint! The higher north summit is 0.4 mile from the first peak of Mount Ripinsky. The return compass course between the peaks is 120 degrees.

# SEVEN MILE SADDLE AND HAINES HIGHWAY

**TIME:** 8.5–9 hours
**DISTANCE:** 9.5 miles
**ELEVATION GAIN:** 5,050 feet

The ridge walk from Haines, over Mount Ripinsky, to Seven Mile Saddle and Haines Highway, makes a long day. Take along the Ten Essentials and plan in advance for return road transportation to town.

A late-summer melt pool is found almost at the lowest point along the ridge, otherwise the ridge is dry. There is a short scramble over loose rock on the climb to the final peak. There are good camping sites on the saddle above Seven Mile Saddle and Haines Highway, and a trickle of water crosses the trail at the south end of the saddle.

The trail is not immediately obvious from the north summit of Mount Ripinsky, so follow the summit ridge for almost 0.25 mile and look for trail wands descending to the right. From here the route should present no difficulties in clear weather. Those traveling in the other direction, southeast from the ridge onto Mount Ripinsky, should take a compass course of 148 degrees (true) from the last wands, if they meet bad weather.

From "Peak 3920" there is a steep descent to Seven Mile Saddle. Beware of avalanche conditions in spring. The trail wanders through alpine parkland to the south end of the saddle, then drops off through brush into the trees. It then follows a small stream for a short distance, and ends at the road about 0.1 mile east of milepost 7 and a rifle range. Allow 4.5 hours or more from Mount Ripinsky down to the road, and those going south allow 3.5 hours from the road to "Peak 3920."

## H2
# MOUNT RILEY AND BATTERY POINT COMPLEX

**TIME:** 2 hours by short route
**DISTANCE:** 2.1 miles from Mud Bay Road
**ELEVATION GAIN:** 1,760 feet
**RATING:** moderate
**TYPE:** shoreline, forest
**MAPS:** Skagway A-1 and A-2
Battery Point has access difficulties

Mount Riley, the highest point on the Chilkat Peninsula south of Haines, lies within the Chilkat State Park and is a moderately easy hike for families. The summit gives extensive views of the Chilkat River flats, Taiya Inlet, Katzehin River, Lynn Canal, and a distant view of town. Often northern harriers, goshawks, bald eagles, and ravens soar on thermals over the summit. The route from Mud Bay Road is the shortest, and the one via Battery Point the prettiest. The best day's walk is up from Portage Cove by Battery Point, and down by Lily Lake.

The shortest and simplest route follows the Mud Bay Road south of town, from Port Chilkoot to the top of the second steep hill, just short of milepost 3. The marked trail starts on top of a steep bank, on the left side of the road across from a parking place. It runs east and meets the Lily Lake Road trail about 0.5 mile after a short climb. Turn right, cross a stream, and climb for about 1 mile through forest to open muskeg on top. Do not turn back here thinking this is the end. The views on top are too good to miss. Cross by the planks, and continue in semi-open country for 0.1 mile to the viewpoint on the final summit.

*Chilkat River from Mount Riley*

# MOUNT RILEY VIA LILY LAKE

**TIME:** 3 hours
**DISTANCE:** 3.8 miles
**ELEVATION GAIN:** same

Walk from Port Chilkoot's "Officers' Row" southward along the FAA Road to its end, about 1 mile (see map). Take the Haines city water supply access road towards Lily Lake to a trail turnoff on the right, about 2 miles or 50 minutes walking time. If it is hard to find, walk to the lake, then retrace your steps for 200 yards looking for trail tread on the left. Once through the initial brush, it is not hard to follow. Five minutes of walking leads to the main trail from Mud Bay Road. This is a pleasant intermediate ski route in winter. (Note: this access is by courtesy of the city of Haines. Please stay away from the lake and do not disturb city property.)

# BATTERY POINT TRAIL

**TIME:** 1 hour, 3 hours to Mount Riley
**DISTANCE:** 2 miles, 5.5 miles to Mount Riley
**ELEVATION GAIN:** insignificant to beach, 1,760 feet to Mount Riley

This is a 2-mile shoreline route maintained partly by Haines Borough and partly by Chilkat State Park. It starts from the end of Beach Road at the south end of Portage Cove. Battery and Kelgaya points provide picnic beaches and primitive camping and are also reached by canoe or kayak. Despite destruction of the original trail by borough property sales, foot passage rights are guaranteed. For the time being, take the road for 0.7 mile, about 10 to 15 minutes. When it is possible, go left to find the original trail, which parallels the road. Do not be deterred by "Keep Out" signs.

Watch for a trail junction after almost 2 miles. Keep straight, across a small stream, to reach the beach west of Kelgaya Point. If one stays quiet, many water birds, such as goldeneye, three types of scoter, harlequin, and bufflehead, are often seen rafting in the shallow tidal waters. There is camping behind both points and views up and down the Lynn Canal.

At the junction, turn right for Mount Riley summit, 3.7 miles

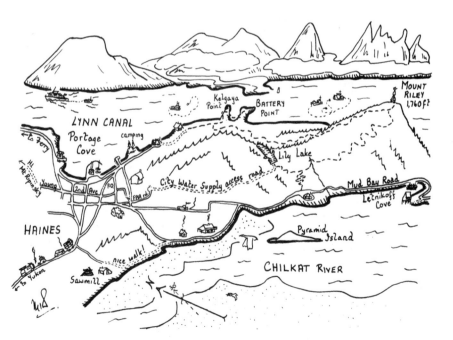

*Bald eagle in flight (Photo by R. T. Wallen)*

away. Lily Lake, over the top, is 5.2 miles from this junction. The climb is steep at first, then more gentle as the route follows the ridge over Half Dome. Watch for moose in the thick blueberries along the ridge. The main trail is joined at the muskeg on top. Turn left for the summit viewpoint. It is possible to lose this trail when snow is on the ground. Take a compass and extra food just in case.

Allow at least 5.5 hours, if the intent is to walk from Mud Bay Road over Mount Riley, and end in town via Portage Cove and Battery Point.

# H3
# SEDUCTION POINT

**TIME:** 4–5 hours or overnight
**DISTANCE:** 6.5 miles
**ELEVATION GAIN:** insignificant
**RATING:** easy to moderate
**TYPE:** intertidal shoreline
**MAPS:** Skagway A-1 and A-2
Tide tables needed

Seduction Point is on the southern tip of the Chilkat Peninsula, in Chilkat State Park. This shoreline walk offers outstanding views of the Davidson Glacier across Chilkat Inlet. The bird and sea life is prolific,

*Mount Davidson from Twin Coves*

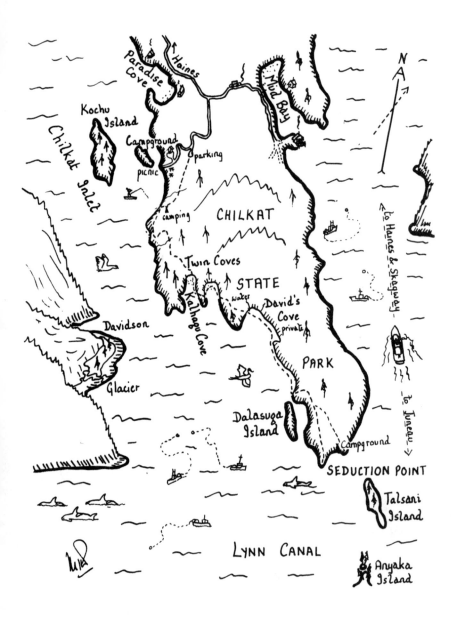

with the possibility of sighting seals, sea lions, porpoises, and humpback and killer whales. Enjoy the brilliant yellows of buttercups, the blues of lupines, and the reds of aquilegia carpet in the first 2 miles of the upper shoreline in high summer.

The trail is good for family groups, because the walk can be long or short as desired. Drinking water is scarce along the way, but may be found near campsites after 1.4 miles, and in the east cove of Twin Coves. Camping is also available above the cove east of Seduction Point. Take a tide book and plan to walk the last long beach stretch after David's Cove during low or mid-tide. Look carefully for trail markers and interpretive signs in the tall grass.

Drive south from Port Chilkoot along Mud Bay Road. Turn right for Chilkat State Park after 5.7 miles (see map). Park in the turnaround at the last S bend of the steep hill or at the picnic grounds at the end of the road. Either walk 1 mile of brushed trail through the spruce and hemlock forest from the parking area, or walk the beach from the picnic grounds. Just beyond the first rocky point, the trail leaves the beach and runs through forest. It then cuts across to Kalhagu Cove (Twin Coves) and again to David's Cove, which is private land on the southerly beach. Stay on the beach to Dalasuga Island, where a land trail might once more be found to Seduction Point. Check the tides beforehand for the long beach walk: the going is rough on the headland behind the beach.

# JUNEAU

JUNEAU, Alaska's capitol, sits on the hemskirts of the Coastal Range Icecap. In April people can stand in the middle of town and watch avalanches topple down the gullies. Yet, only a few weeks later, the deep mountain valleys are bursting with cottonwood fragrance, and bird song fills the air. Hungry bears emerging from their winter sleep come into town for a quick cookie fix in carelessly stowed garbage, until they are chased out by the townsfolk.

Frontage is on protected tidal waters with West Juneau and the city of Douglas facing Juneau. Trade and access is by sea and air since there is no road connection to the Alaskan Highway. Lack of space, due to scant flat land between mountains and sea, dictates Juneau's expansion, and the Mendenhall Valley is the one place where development has occurred. A city bus connects Juneau with Douglas and serves the airport and Auke Bay on an hourly basis. The bus serves the Mendenhall Valley every 2 hours. There is no service to the ferry terminal (13 miles northwest of town). Bus schedules can be picked up at the airport, libraries, and many places in town. There are two USFS campgrounds, one southwest of Mendenhall Glacier, and the other at Auke Bay, 1.6 miles north of the ferry terminal.

History buffs will be pleased to note that Juneau was founded on the discovery of gold in the 1880s, and anyone interested in that era will have a field day hiking the trails. Even place names reflect those times—Bullion Creek, Last Chance Basin, Silverbow Basin, Nugget Creek, and Gold Creek. However, a resurgence of mining in the valleys close to Juneau has led to a rash of trail closures for various reasons. The most notorious and traumatic was the closure of the Flume for "safety reasons." A heartrending cry from the people who had walked the Flume safely for years brought about a happy outcome. Rights of passage were restored to all comers. The Flume is probably the best short walk there is in Juneau. It runs from Basin Road, under Mount Juneau, to the north end of town. (Check the maps carefully. The north end may be found on one of them.)

For more information on trail origins obtain a copy of *In the Miners' Footsteps* written by Willette Janes for the Juneau-Douglas City Museum. Those interested in short strolls and public access areas refer to *90 Short Walks Around Juneau* by Mary Lou King.

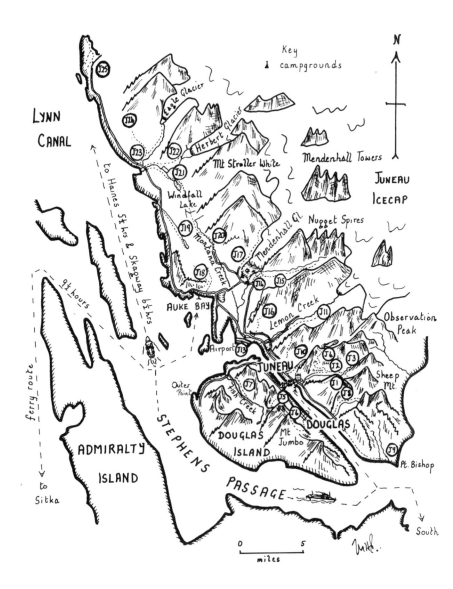

For visitors new to the area and those hesitant to wander off on their own, the Juneau Parks and Recreation Department offers hikes twice a week, which include a mixed bag of easy walks and strenuous, challenging days on the ridges. The department's telephone number is 586-5226 and includes a recorded message after office hours. Hike destinations are also announced over KTOO-FM radio and in the newspaper. Summer hike schedules can be obtained from the borough office during office hours. Car pooling is encouraged, to enable hikers without cars to visit remote areas.

*Hikes from downtown Juneau:* J1 Mount Roberts, J2 Perseverance, J3 Mount Juneau, and J4 Granite Creek Basin offer hiking opportunities within walking distance of downtown Juneau.

*Hikes on Douglas Island:* On his visit to the island in 1794, Captain George Vancouver named Douglas Island (for John Douglas, Bishop of Salisbury, in England). The huge Treadwell Mine made Douglas the largest town in the territory at one time, with over 2,000 souls. Few remains of the mine complex are seen today. A 1917 cave-in killed many miners, and subsequent sea water flooding stopped production. Paris Creek tumbles with a final flourish into a huge, open "glory hole," a relic of open pit mining. Now, seven decades later, the area is a great attraction to visitors and can be seen from the picnic grounds at Sandy Beach. See local publications for further details, or check the Centennial Hall and Log Cabin in downtown Juneau for a pamphlet describing the area.

Douglas Island routes include J5 Dan Moller Ski Trail, J6 Mount Jumbo, and J7 Treadwell Ditch. North Douglas offers a downhill and cross-country ski bowl at Eaglecrest (see J7 Treadwell Ditch; turn left at milepost 7, North Douglas Highway) and many summer walks through alpine meadows to ridgetop. There is also a memorable beach walk at Outer Point, the westernmost tip of Douglas Island.

*Hikes from Juneau's Thane Road:* J8 Sheep Creek and J9 Bishop Point, both south of Juneau, are reached via Thane Road.

*Walks northwest of Juneau:* J10 through J25 are all in the proximity of the airport and Mendenhall Glacier.

# MOUNT ROBERTS

**TIME:** 3 hours
**DISTANCE:** 3.5 miles from waterfront
**ELEVATION GAIN:** 4,210 feet
**RATING:** strenuous
**ACCESS:** foot from town
**TYPE:** alpine
**TRAIL CONDITION:** good, wet in places
**MAPS:** Juneau B-1 and B-2, 1:63,360, or Juneau vicinity, 1:24,000, 2.6
   inch:1 mile (preferable)
Beware of cornicing and avalanche on ridge
Ice ax required for winter travel

The hulk of Mount Roberts sits over Juneau and Sheep Creek like
a crouching bear. A well-used trail climbs its spine and stops short 1
mile from Mount Roberts on the summit of Gastineau Peak. Well-

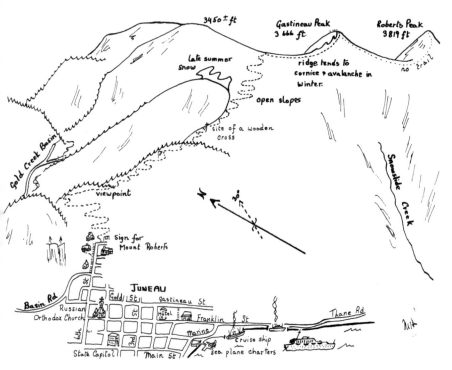

*Juneau from Gastineau Peak*

prepared, experienced hikers can go on from here along the ridge
over Sheep Mountain, to link up with the Sheep Creek trail (J8). Anyone who climbs above treeline has commanding views of the city, the
channel, Douglas Island, and surrounding mountains. For those with
less time, a viewpoint opens up about 200 feet above the trailhead. For
these reasons, and perhaps because the west end of Gastineau Peak is
relatively safe in snow conditions, this is one of the most popular alpine routes in the Juneau district. Those traveling along the ridge in
winter and spring should have ice axes. This route is maintained by
the state of Alaska, but is very wet in places.

From downtown Juneau, take Main, Seward, or Franklin street up
the hill to Sixth Street. Turn right and climb another steep hill to the
end of the street where a Mount Roberts trail sign is seen between two
houses. The path climbs steeply in a series of zigzags onto the wooded
ridge that dominates this end of town, and to the first viewpoint. From
here it climbs steadily, passing one stream on the way up, and finally
breaks out of trees at 1,600 feet. About 300 feet up a steep bank is
where most people pause for a cookie stop before continuing the
climb or returning to town. From here, there are uninterrupted views
of the harbor traffic, the cities of Juneau and Douglas, and surrounding
mountains.

The route climbs steadily onto the broad back of Gastineau Peak, then runs southeast across a fairly narrow, airy ridge to the highest point of the peak, 3,666 feet elevation. Few people venture any farther than this, because the ridge drops 400 feet before continuing to Mount Roberts, 3,819 feet.

## SHEEP MOUNTAIN TRAVERSE

**TIME:** 8 hours from Juneau to Thane
**DISTANCE:** 10 miles
**ELEVATION GAIN:** 5,300 feet
No trail in alpine section
Carry an ice ax

Those interested in extending their hike to a long day or overnight can follow the open ridge above Sheep Creek Basin to Sheep Mountain, 4,238 feet elevation, and descend to Thane (see J8). A wary eye must be kept on the weather because of possible route-finding difficulties to the upper end of the Sheep Creek Trail. In good weather it should be fairly easy to locate where the Annex Creek powerlines cross the ridge about 1.5 miles southeast of Sheep Mountain. The descending trail may be found close to the powerlines at about the 2,300-foot level.

# J2
# PERSEVERANCE

**TIME:** 2.5 hours from town
**DISTANCE:** 2.5 miles (4 miles from town)
**ELEVATION GAIN:** 1,100 feet
**RATING:** easy
**ACCESS:** foot from Juneau
**TYPE:** historical, scenic valley
**MAPS:** Juneau B-2 1:63,360 or Juneau vicinity, 1:24,000, 2.6 inch:1
    mile (preferable). Maps are not necessary for those staying on
    trail.
Avalanche danger, subject to periodic slides and closures

Perseverance is probably the most popular walk around town. The old roadway is used by joggers, Sunday strollers, dog walkers, historians, gold panners, and serious hikers.

This beautiful valley gives access to Mount Juneau, Silverbow

Basin, and Granite Creek Basin. The approach is through a steep gorge along Basin Road, part of which is trestle, overhanging Gold Creek. In early spring the first bears of the season are seen grazing on the opposite mountain slope, and fine filigreed waterfalls float down the rock walls of Mount Juneau. At this time the distinctive fragrance of cottonwoods titillate the senses, and warbler chatter and thrush cadences fill the gorge with sound. Visitors should park their cars in town and walk up Basin Road (1.5 miles) because the road is narrow, and the gorge can be seen better on foot.

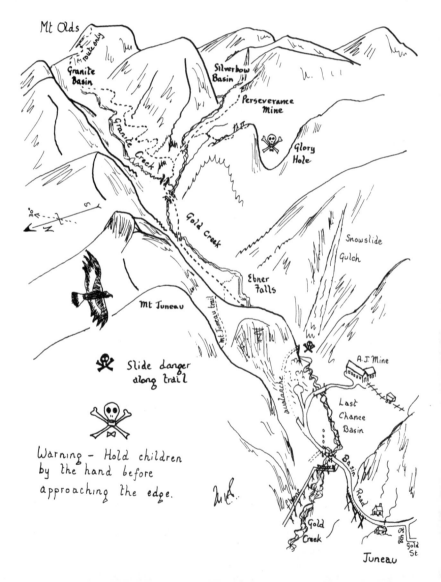

The trail was originally a wagon road built into the sheer-walled mountain in the 1880s, shortly after Joe Juneau discovered gold in Last Chance Basin at the end of Basin Road. Remains of the Alaska-Juneau (A-J) Mine are terraced up the steep hillside. A horizontal mine shaft is visible at the Perseverance trailhead, and a Pelton wheel, which was working during the mine's heyday, has been placed here for general interest. A self-guided historical tour of the mine buildings is highly recommended for the casual visitor. Conversely, the huge Perseverance Mine complex in Silverbow Basin has almost totally disappeared, but "glory holes" (open vertical shafts) still remain. Take care when hiking off the road to avoid concealed holes scattered throughout the area. Watch for the Flume, which takes off to the left where Basin Road crosses Gold Creek. The Perseverance Trail, and others in the same valley, are maintained by the state.

From the town center, walk up Main Street past the Capitol building, and turn right onto Sixth Street. Take the next left, uphill onto Gold Street. A right at the road end, followed by a left, leads onto Basin Road. Walk past the last houses, along the trestle, across Gold Creek to

*Looking east from Mount Juneau*

a fork in the road. The right fork descends to Gold Creek and the entrance to the A-J Mine. Take the left fork, which also drops downhill to the trailhead.

The trail climbs steeply for a short distance before joining the original wagon road. Half a mile from the road fork is a viewpoint of Snowslide Gulch; after another 0.5 mile, Ebner Falls is visible. The trail up Mount Juneau (J3) is opposite the upper end of the falls. A mile farther along Perseverance trail, shortly after the miner's road crosses Granite Creek, a well-defined trail to the left gives access to Granite Creek Basin and Mount Olds (J4). About 0.4 mile up the valley, a spur trail to the right leads to the Glory Hole, a man-made pit 220 feet deep and 100 yards across. Some ruined mine buildings may be found in the area. Do not let children approach the edge alone. The main trail ends in Silverbow Basin under an immense cirque of mountains, and scattered remains of the Perseverance Mine may still be found in the surrounding brush.

Warning: avalanche danger is high during winter and early spring. Mud slides are liable to occur after heavy rains, with slippage possible along the first mile of trail.

# J3
# MOUNT JUNEAU

**TIME:** 3 hours
**DISTANCE:** 4 miles from town center
**ELEVATION GAIN:** 3,576 feet
**RATING:** strenuous
**ACCESS:** Perseverance trail (J2)
**TYPE:** alpine
**MAPS:** Juneau B-2, 1:63,360 or Juneau vicinity, 1:24,000, 2.6 inch:1
   mile (preferable)
Serious avalanche danger, ice ax required winter and spring

Mount Juneau dominates town to the north. The sleeping winter giant awakens with a roar in spring as avalanches tumble down the gullies with enough noise to stop the downtown shoppers in their tracks—warning enough to not go up too early. An ice ax is needed into June for steep, hard snow-covered gullies and upper slopes. Later in the year, it is a steep, yet rewarding climb. The summit panorama is

superb, with views of the town and tidal waters and across Douglas Is-
land to Admiralty Island. On clear days Mount Crillon, 12,700 feet, and
Mount Fairweather, 15,300 feet, can be seen on the western side of
Glacier Bay, about 100 miles away.

The trail starts at the upper end of Ebner Falls, half a mile along
the Perseverance trail (J2). It climbs fairly steeply through slide alder,
then briefly through a grove of hemlock trees to the top of a mountain
rib, called the Horn. From here, at about 1,200 feet elevation, the path
traverses almost a mile across steep open slopes with good views of
Juneau, and the A-J Mine directly below. Keep eyes open for a flooded
horizontal mine shaft along this section. In early summer, hard snow
may be found across the steep stream gullies, and some can only be
crossed safely with an ice ax and safety line. If wet, parts of the trail
can be very slippery and difficult to negotiate. The route runs by a
coppice and climbs steeply onto open slopes to the summit.

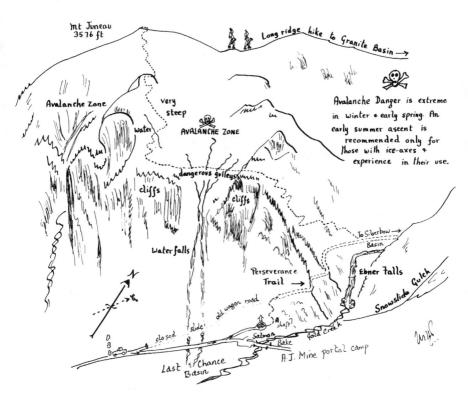

## TRAVERSE TO GRANITE CREEK BASIN

**TIME:** 8–10 hours round trip
**DISTANCE:** 10.6 miles
**ELEVATION GAIN:** 4,400 feet
Route only

Strong hikers with practice in cross-country navigation can keep going eastward along the ridge towards Mount Olds, then drop down into Granite Creek Basin (J4). The traverse is airy and beautiful. It is not difficult, just very long. Be sure to take along survival gear (the Ten Essentials) because of exposure to sudden weather changes. A cooking stove is necessary for overnight camping.

J4
# GRANITE CREEK BASIN

**TIME:** 3 hours from town
**DISTANCE:** 3.6 miles
**ELEVATION GAIN:** 1,700 ± feet
**RATING:** moderate
**ACCESS:** Perseverance trail (J2)
**TYPE:** alpine bowl
**MAPS:** Juneau B-1 and B-2 or Juneau vicinity 1:24,000, 2.6 inch:1 mile
(preferred)
Avalanche danger

Granite Creek Basin is an alpine bowl under Mount Olds. In late summer it is carpeted with flowers; look for blue cranesbill (wild geranium), forget-me-not (Alaska's state flower), delicate clusters of western columbine peeping out from under moss-covered rocks, and white grass of Parnassus. Growing in profusion on both the Granite Creek Basin and Perseverance trails are monkshood, bluebells, and yellow arnica. Granite Creek cascades down the ledges of the basin into Gold Creek.

A trip extension to Mount Olds (see below) opens up the ice cap scenery with views of the Devils Paw, the Norris Glacier, Taku Inlet, and the deep cleft of Carlson Creek.

Follow Perseverance trail (J2) 1.6 miles to Granite Creek. A few yards farther on, turn left at the trail division and climb the hill up the side valley. To get into the lower basin in late spring, kick steps into the hard snow to the right of the cascading creek. Snow may linger in the upper basin until late August. Once in the basin above the first Granite Creek cataract, a spillover of a natural pool, the path disappears. But from here the walking is easy; the upper bowl 0.7 mile away at 2,200 feet elevation.

## MOUNT OLDS

**TIME:** 5 hours from town
**DISTANCE:** 4.5 miles
**ELEVATION GAIN:** 4,453 feet
Route only

Continue onto Mount Olds by climbing up steep heather and grass slopes onto the west ridge. From here there is easy scrambling onto the summit, but prepare for a trouble-free descent by closely noting the route. The south ridge looks tempting from below, but route-finding is not easy through the rock buttresses.

## J5
# DAN MOLLER SKI TRAIL

**TIME:** 1.5 hours
**DISTANCE:** 3.2 miles (4.8 miles from downtown Juneau)
**ELEVATION GAIN:** 1,800 feet
**RATING:** moderate
**ACCESS:** bus to West Juneau or foot from town
**TYPE:** muskeg meadows
**TRAIL CONDITION:** Boardwalk
**MAP:** Juneau B-2 or Juneau vicinity, 1:24,000 (recommended)
Overnight ski cabin

Late summer, fields of Alaska bog cotton turn the muskegs white, and the ridges above become a mellow gold from the dying deer cabbage. Mount Troy rises on the west side of Kowee Basin (named after an Auke Indian chief), and it is a good vantage point for the Admiralty

Island peaks. However, equally good views can be obtained by climbing the extra 500 feet directly to the ridge, southwest of the trail end. The ski cabin, located in the upper basin, was originally built in 1936 and rebuilt by local volunteers in 1983. It has a warming stove and plenty of bunk space. Take a cooking stove and leave a clean cabin. Carry out all unused food and garbage so as not to attract bears. The trail and cabin are administered by the USFS.

If walking the extra 1.6 miles from Juneau, go across the Douglas Bridge to West Juneau; turn left, then right up Cordova Street to its

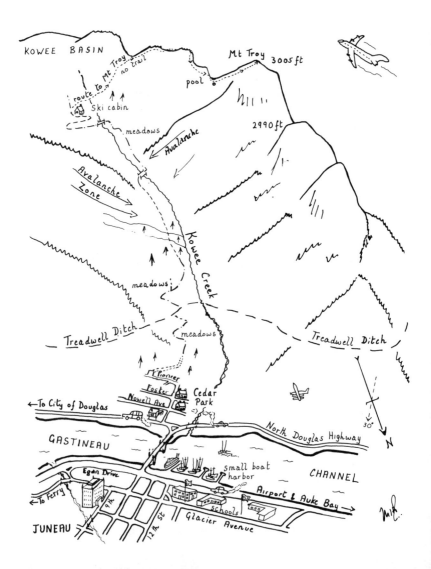

end. Turn left onto Pioneer, and within a quarter of a mile the Dan Moller parking lot appears on the right. The Douglas bus will take passengers from town to Cordova Street. The trail is wide and easy to follow. Much of it is boardwalk through wet open meadows, although the boards can become extremely slippery when icy or wet. About half a mile from the beginning, watch for the Treadwell Ditch.

## MOUNT TROY

**TIME:** 3.5 hours
**DISTANCE:** 4.2 miles
**ELEVATION GAIN:** 3,005 feet
No trail

To continue up Mount Troy from the end of trail, climb to the ridgetop to the left of the peak. Descend to a notch and go left past a small pond, then go up a steep open slope to the summit ridge. If a

*Eagle Peak, Admiralty Island from Mount Troy*

right turn is made in the notch, there is a scramble through brush and a fight with small trees. Good luck with the trees; they are a delight. From here it is easy slab scrambling to the summit.

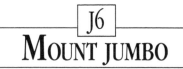

# J6
# MOUNT JUMBO

**TIME:** 3.5 hours
**DISTANCE:** 2.6 miles
**ELEVATION GAIN:** 3,337 feet
**RATING:** strenuous
**ACCESS:** bus or car to Douglas (3.5 miles)
**TYPE:** forest, alpine
**TRAIL CONDITION:** fair
**MAPS:** A-2 and B-2, or Juneau vicinity 1:24,000 (recommended)

Mount Bradley is the name on the map, but Mount Jumbo (named for the shape of the peak when viewed from Sheep Creek) is the colloquial appellation. The peak rises above Douglas and commands sweeping views of Juneau, Gastineau Inlet, and Admiralty Island. Part of the lower end of the trail is owned by the A-J Industries, yet public access is allowed. The path is wet and muddy at first, but it enters open muskeg after about a mile and 550 feet of climbing, with views south to Taku Inlet. If this is as far as the casual walker goes, it is worth the trip. Waterproof boots are recommended.

The posted trail starts between the 300 and 400 blocks on Fifth Street in Douglas. It climbs through new growth forest, then runs along an old mine feeder ditch before reaching Paris Creek. (The creek plunges into a gorge immediately below the trail. The falls can be viewed from a short, steep spur that should be negotiated with care.) The main route follows the creek briefly uphill, crosses it, and continues to climb to the Treadwell Ditch. From here, a boardwalk shows the way to the base of the mountain. Where the trail re-enters the trees, it becomes steep and rough once more to gain access to the ridge.

As the trees thin, views of Juneau, surrounding mountains, and tidal waters open up. A small stream may be encountered (depending on the time of year) shortly before the path emerges from the trees.

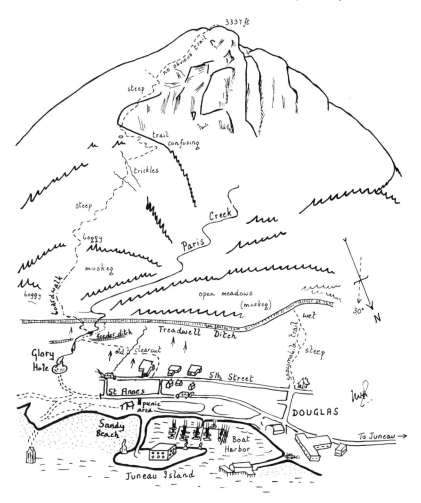

When the trail reaches alpine and open ridge, note the direction and position for the way down. The final summit towers about 1,000 feet above this point. The ridge encircles Paris Creek basin, and an ice ax is recommended while snow lingers on exposed slopes. The summit is sprinkled with alpine tarns, many half covered with snow into August.

### J7

# TREADWELL DITCH

## EAGLECREST TO DAN MOLLER (J5)

**TIME:** 7 hours
**DISTANCE:** 12 miles
**ELEVATION GAIN/LOSS:** 250 feet
**RATING:** easy to moderate
**ACCESS:** bus to West Juneau, car to Eaglecrest
**TYPE:** historical, forest
**TRAIL CONDITION:** mostly good
**MAP:** Juneau B-2 (Juneau vicinity for south end, 2.6 inch:1 mile)

The Treadwell Ditch was completed in 1890. It was designed to drain the water from upper Fish Creek and all north Douglas side streams to Paris Creek for the stamp mills and waterwheels of the day. Most of the mine buildings in Douglas disappeared, some in 1917,

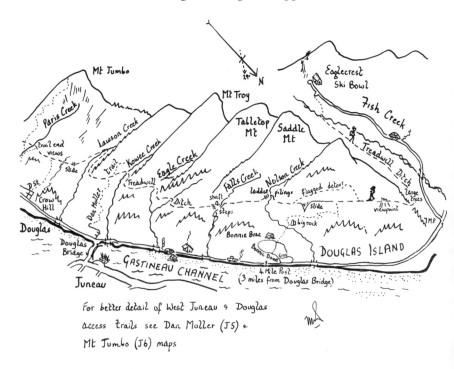

For better detail of West Juneau & Douglas access trails see Dan Moller (J5) & Mt Jumbo (J6) maps

after a disastrous tidal water cave-in, but the ditch remains as a reminder of mining activity. The walk along the ditch is of quiet beauty and sustained interest. The structure itself is of real interest to those knowledgeable in the construction of log flumes. The walk along the ditch is kept open by the USFS, and it was last brushed in 1981. Porcupine may be seen along the trail, and be alert to the shrill whistle of marmots and the occasional black bear (brown bear are generally not found on Douglas Island). The views downslope are limited by forest in the upper reaches of the hike, except for one viewpoint overlooking the Lemon Creek tidal flats. At lower elevations, side valleys offer views of open muskeg and ridgetops.

One can either walk short distances and turn back or arrange for a car at both ends of the trip and walk the entire ditch. There is one bad slide that requires a diversion above the trail (not well marked), and one or two wet and muddy places where boots would be helpful. (Most of the approaches are wet and muddy also.) The ditch makes a good cross-country ski outing in winter for intermediate skiers.

There are five major access routes onto the Treadwell Ditch between Fish Creek and Paris Creek. First, the origin in Fish Creek is about 0.1 mile north of the Eaglecrest ski lifts and road end, 11.4 miles west of Juneau, or 4.4 miles from the North Douglas Highway. From Juneau, cross the Douglas Bridge and turn right. At milepost 7 (5.9 miles north of the Douglas Bridge), turn left and drive up the road to Eaglecrest Ski Bowl. In summer, a boardwalk is visible on the left side of the road by a small parking area. The boardwalk descends toward Fish Creek, with wet open patches in places and a steep staircase to a bridge across the stream. The ditch is on the other side.

The second approach is from Bonnie Brae housing development. Turn right off the Douglas bridge and go north 3.2 miles (0.2 mile beyond milepost 4). Turn left up Bonnie Doon and right up Margarita to the far end, before the road loops back. Look for a plank across the ditch; the trail leads into the trees between two houses. The path goes through two open muskegs before going back into trees and crossing Neilson Creek. It then climbs fairly steeply and partially traverses the hillside northward until it meets an old trail at a T junction. Turn left up the hill and climb to the ditch, which will be found close to some ruins. Turn right along the ditch to meet the trail from Eaglecrest. From here, look for markers and tread leading uphill on the left for the slide bypass and the southward route to West Juneau. Careful routefinding is needed to stay on the bypass.

Another approach is via the Dan Moller Ski Trail (J5) from West Juneau. Look for the ditch shortly after ascending the first muskeg, 700

*Treadwell Ditch*

feet elevation, with views of Juneau. The trail briefly follows the ditch, although it can be missed if the signpost is gone, and it has not been brushed recently.

# TREADWELL DITCH AND PARIS CREEK TO DAN MOLLER SKI TRAIL (J5)

**TIME:** 3 hours
**DISTANCE:** 5 miles
**ELEVATION GAIN:** 700 feet
**ACCESS:** bus to Douglas or West Juneau
**TRAIL CONDITION:** good
**MAP:** Juneau vicinity, 1:24,000, 2.6 inches:1 mile

The southeast end of the Treadwell Ditch is used in winter by snowmobilers and skiers. Openings in trees offer good views of the mainland mountains and tidal waters. The good trail goes as far as Paris Creek, although the ditch continues southeast to Ready Bullion Creek.

The Mount Jumbo Trail (J6) on Fifth Street in Douglas provides the most southerly and easiest access route onto the Treadwell Ditch. Do not cross Paris Creek. Follow the tiny trail running uphill on the near side of the creek. It emerges into a meadow and disappears, but the ditch will be found directly uphill. Coming down, flagging marks the beginning, but careful route-finding is needed to stay on track. If the trail is lost, follow the creek until the Mount Jumbo Trail is seen. When the ditch is reached, turn right to ascend to the crossing of the Dan Moller Ski Trail.

Another way onto the ditch is from the north end of Fifth Street in Douglas. When approaching Douglas from Juneau, turn right onto D Street, a one-way street at its upper end. A jeep trail goes steeply uphill from Fifth Street as a continuation of D Street. This is used by snow-mobilers and skiers in winter, and in summer it is bog toward the top. On good days the views of Gastineau Channel are open and worth the short, steep, sloppy walk.

# J8
# SHEEP CREEK

**TIME:** 1.5 hours
**DISTANCE:** 2.2 miles
**ELEVATION GAIN:** 800 feet
**RATING:** moderate
**ACCESS:** 3.5 miles south of Juneau
**TYPE:** valley, alpine, historical
**TRAIL CONDITION:** good first 2 miles; poor to ridge
**MAPS:** Juneau B-1 or Juneau vicinity 1:24,000, 2.6 inch:1 mile (recommended)
Avalanche danger

The Sheep Creek canyon is a narrow, steep-sided defile that bustled with mining activity in the late 1880s. It got its name when the first miners mistook the mountain goats they saw on the crags for sheep. Renewal of mining activity threatens this wild valley with promises of tailing heaps large enough to dam the river. This would

*Mining remains on Sheep Creek*

mean the end of the trail and the valley as we know it. A road has been built into Portal Camp, 1.5 miles up the valley, and a small trailer camp has been placed on-site. Hikers are advised to stay away from private property. Many old relics still lie undisturbed within the valley portal. The trail is maintained by the state.

Strong hikers with expertise in high-level cross-country travel can enjoy a full day to ridgetop, Sheep Mountain, or even to Juneau over the tops. Beware of ridge cornicing on Mount Roberts and Gastineau Peak. The steep climb out of the valley is passable, though not regularly brushed.

From the center of Juneau, drive southeast along the shoreline road, Thane Road, to milepost 4. A few yards before the main road crosses Sheep Creek, a short spur goes to a powerhouse on the left. The trail, which starts with a staircase, is on the hill side of the junction. Parking is available at the trailhead.

The trail climbs steeply at first, to about 600 feet above the river gorge. Then it drops into the valley, where the going is easy and pleas-

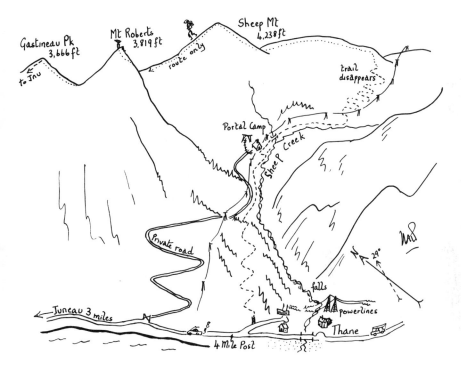

ant on a broad pathway. The river here is a boiling cataract, and dippers (small brown water ouzel) are often seen bobbing on the rocks or walking into the water in search of food. Powerlines from Annex Creek to Thane also run up the valley, and the trail follows them closely as it zigzags to the ridge.

# SHEEP MOUNTAIN

**TIME:** 5.5 hours
**DISTANCE:** 5 miles
**ELEVATION GAIN:** 4,238 feet
**RATING:** strenuous
No trail on ridgetop

Follow the trail northeast under the powerlines to the ridge. The climb is steep, and brush may be a problem, so note well where the path emerges from the trees at about 2,600 feet for the return. Go northwest to climb Sheep Mountain, which dominates the skyline in this direction. In good weather, hiking to the broad ridge should present no difficulties. The reward is a view of the entire length of the deep valley left behind. Mount Hawthorne is a striking peak to the southeast. Be sure to have foul-weather gear and the Ten Essentials for walking in high country.

---

## J9
# BISHOP POINT (DUPONT)

**TIME:** 4.5 hours
**DISTANCE:** 8 miles
**ELEVATION GAIN:** 200 feet
**RATING:** moderate
**ACCESS:** Thane Road, 6 miles south of Juneau
**TYPE:** forest, shoreline
**TRAIL CONDITION:** fair, muddy
**MAPS:** Juneau A-1 and B-1

The main interest of this trail is tidal fishing at Dupont, a wharf and powder magazine in 1917, situated 1.7 miles from the road head. In the past people could fish directly off the dock, but it has seen better days. Now Dolly Varden trout and the occasional salmon are caught directly off the rocks. However, as a result of its popularity the path to Dupont is overworn, with exposed tree roots and mud holes. The route hugs the shore most of the way to Bishop Point, and it crosses two raging mountain torrents (Grindstone and Rhine creeks) about 6.5 and 7 miles from the road. Powerlines from Snettisham have been relocated to the hillside directly above the trail. They interfere with the trail about 1.5 miles south of Dupont, where there are some 150 yards of poor pathway with windfalls and encroaching brush. Do not be surprised to meet windfalls in other places along the route. Otherwise, it offers quiet forest and shoreline with many beautiful side streams and arching canopies of devil's club (don't touch!).

Drive or bicycle to the end of Thane Road, 6 miles southeast of Juneau, and take the trail that starts from the parking area. Almost immediately it crosses Little Sheep Creek. About half a mile before reaching Dupont, the path to Bishop Point leads off to the left and climbs a 200-foot hill, crossing Dupont Creek above the powder house ruins. It then drops down into moss-covered forests and carpets of deer cabbage, which glow yellow in late summer. At the end of trail (it used to go to Annex Creek in Taku Inlet), a vandalized cabin stands on the west shoreline of Bishop Point.

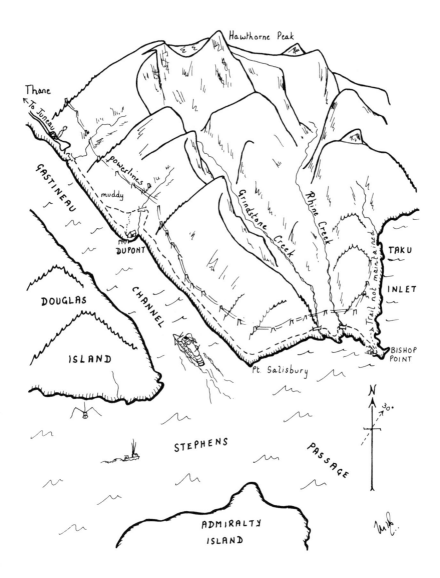

*Devil's club*

# J10
# SALMON CREEK

**TIME:** 2.5 hours
**DISTANCE:** 3.5 miles
**ELEVATION GAIN:** 1,200 feet
**RATING:** moderate (easy first 2 miles)
**ACCESS:** 3 miles northwest of Juneau
**TYPE:** forest, historical, reservoir
**TRAIL CONDITION:** excellent
**MAPS:** Juneau B-1 or Juneau vicinity (not needed for those staying on road)
Steep staircase toward end presents a danger to children

Caught within the bowl formed by Cairn Peak, Observation Peak, and Mount Olds, lies the Salmon Creek Reservoir built in the early 1900s. At about the same time, a tramway was built to haul up supplies, and it can still be seen today. Salmon Creek, or Tilhini "the dog salmon," its original Native name, becomes locked within a narrow, steep-sided valley bounded by Mount Juneau on the southeast and Blackerby Ridge to the northwest on its way to the sea. A road to the powerhouse was constructed in 1984 to replace the dangerous, but picturesque, trestle tramway and flume. Access to hikers is allowed through Alaska Electric Light and Power (AEL&P) property, which is administered by the state. AEL&P has recently rebuilt the staircase.

Go north on Egan Drive, 2.3 miles beyond the traffic lights at the Douglas Bridge. Turn right into the Salmon Creek powerhouse grounds and park by the trail sign. The turn is easily missed, so don't panic. Just continue to the next light (0.3 mile) at Salmon Creek. Turn right and park in the Twin Lakes Recreation Area on the left side of the road immediately after crossing the creek. Walk back along the bicycle

*Mount Olds from Salmon Creek Reservoir Dam*

trail. (Those walking from town can also follow the same bicycle trail at the end of the old Glacier Highway.)

Salmon Creek Trail starts as a dirt service road that climbs steeply above the river and ends at the upper powerhouse 2 miles away. Shortly after the road crosses Salmon Creek, look for a trail going off to the left into trees. It joins with the old tramway, which parallels the road and climbs very gradually through moss-covered forest. After reaching the dam, the route climbs very steeply to the left, through trees, over a series of staircases, to the dam catwalk. This climb is not suitable for small children; it can be dangerous for adults.

The view across the reservoir makes the walk worthwhile, but a gate stops people from getting onto the dam. Observation Peak, 4,935 feet elevation, dominates the cirque above the reservoir. The reservoir gives a bird's-eye view of trees, a huge drop, and the valley reaching down to the sea. There is good brook trout fishing in the reservoir. Some people have gained access onto Blackerby Ridge from the north end of the dam, but it is considered very steep and dangerous and is not recommended.

## J11
# BLACKERBY RIDGE

**TIME:** 2.5 hours
**DISTANCE:** 2 miles
**ELEVATION GAIN:** 3,215 feet
**RATING:** strenuous
**ACCESS:** 3.4 miles northwest of Juneau
**TYPE:** alpine
**TRAIL CONDITION:** primitive path
**MAPS:** Juneau B-2
No trail on ridge

This route is not for beginners. It gives access onto the ridge between Salmon and Lemon creeks, and it is used as one of the major access routes onto the ice cap. Views of the ice cap and surrounding peaks are outstanding from Cairn Peak. Hikers also get extensive vistas of the airport complex and the distant Chilkat Range shortly after emerging from the trail into alpine. The trail starts on private property,

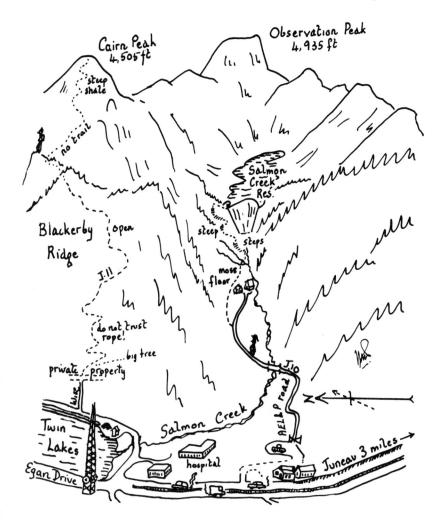

but it is hoped that access rights will be purchased by the city some-time in the future. Hikers are warned to respect the rights of property owners, and permission should be obtained before crossing private land.

Take Egan Drive, the main highway running northwest out of Juneau, and turn right at the first traffic light 2.5 miles after passing Douglas Bridge (Salmon Creek and hospital). Immediately after cross-ing the creek, turn left into the Twin Lakes parking lot. Continue on

foot north along Old Glacier Highway, and turn right up Wire Street to
its end. The trail beginning may be lost due to building activity, but a
primitive footpath is found behind the building sites directly across
from the end of Wire Street. Do not cross private land. Go around. The
footpath climbs steeply uphill through windfalls. At one point it goes
up a steep bank that has a rope as an aid. It continues through heavy
timber to a meadow approximately 1,800 feet elevation. It traverses
the meadow and follows a stream course to another meadow about
200 feet higher. The route goes through small timber, keeping to the
open as much as possible. It disappears shortly after reaching alpine
levels at 2,600 feet. Navigating the ridge is a little tricky. Follow cairns
at first towards the first peak, 3,215 feet above sea level. Be sure to
note where the end of the trail is for the return.

## CAIRN PEAK

**TIME:** 7 hours
**DISTANCE:** 4.5 miles
**ELEVATION GAIN:** 5,100 feet
Route only

Most of the little peaks on the ridge are unavoidable, making it a
rough cross-country walk, but it is worth going east toward Cairn Peak
for expansive views of Ptarmigan Glacier, the upper reaches of Lemon
Creek, and a bird's-eye view of the Salmon Creek Dam. There are many
good relatively sheltered campsites (considering the position) that
have snowmelt pools into early August. Take a cookstove—wood is
scarce—and don't forget the Ten Essentials. The climb onto Cairn
Peak, 4,505 feet above sea level, is steep, with exposed slopes of loose
shale, but is not technically difficult. However, it is only for the sure
footed, and a rope would be handy. When snow covers the final 500
feet, an ice ax and ropes are highly recommended.

## J12
# LEMON CREEK

Lemon Creek trail lies within the Goldbelt Native Land Selection,
and much of the trail has been obliterated. There is a possibility it will
be re-routed by the USFS in the near future.

# J13
# MENDENHALL WETLANDS

**TIME:** 1 hour or more
**DISTANCE:** 2.5 miles from terminal to end of dyke
**ELEVATION GAIN:** none
**RATING:** easy
**ACCESS:** city bus or foot from airport
**TYPE:** tidal wetlands
**TRAIL CONDITION:** excellent

Waiting for a plane? Getting bored? Grab the binoculars and go for a walk. Except for hunting season, the Mendenhall Wetlands is the place to see birds—waterfowl, waders, swans, geese and more. In spring, aggressive courtship is displayed and territorial rights asserted in a riot of song. By mid-June the songs have died down, but nesting season is in full swing. The airport runway and seaplane takeoff ponds have raised dirt roads around the west and south sides that give good views of the tidal marshes. Up here the walking is easy, but take a tide table and wear rubber boots for strolls over the marshes. Beware of

*Trumpeter swan at Mendenhall Wetlands*

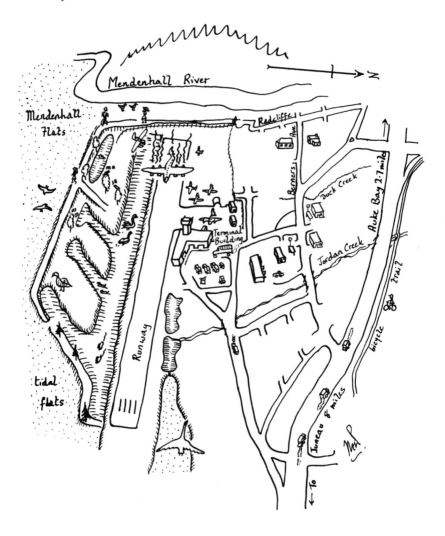

the incoming tide. The hiker can be cut off by back channels, so cross only when the tide is receding. The wetlands have been declared a state game refuge.

The walk can be as long or as short as desired, but allow 20 minutes to get to the west end of the runway, almost a mile from the airport terminal. Turn left outside the terminal building, then left on Old Glacier Highway at two service stations. Turn left again onto Berners Avenue, and left on Radcliffe to a gate at its end. There is a pedestrian right-of-way to one side of the gate and across the end of the runway.

# EAST GLACIER COMPLEX

**TIME:** 2 hours round trip
**DISTANCE:** 3 miles
**ELEVATION GAIN:** 600 feet
**RATING:** easy to moderate
**ACCESS:** Mendenhall Glacier USFS Visitor Center
**TYPE:** glacial recession, glacier and valley views
**TRAIL CONDITION:** good
**MAP:** Juneau B-2, but not necessary for those staying on the trail

This complex of trails, starting from the USFS Visitor Center at the Mendenhall Glacier, affords good sightseeing opportunities of the glacier itself, and the biological reclamation of the valley floor after a recent glacial retreat. Water-filled kettles (hollows) and lichen- and brush-covered kames (hillocks) characterize the flat areas, with willow, sweet smelling cottonwood, and alder. Emerging hemlock and spruce cover the hillslopes.

For spring bird song, this is the place to go. The ambience is shaped by the single quavering, whistled notes of varied thrushes, the chur-r-r-r-r of tiny yellow warblers, ascending triplets of tinier golden-crowned kinglets, the short soulful song of hermit thrushes, and the ascending carillons of Swainson's thrushes.

Turn right at the second set of lights beyond the airport turn, 8.6 miles northwest of Juneau, up the Mendenhall Loop Road to the glacier, 3.6 miles farther on. A 30-minute ecological loop trail winds around the moraine on the valley floor between the parking lot and Mendenhall River. Another nature trail traverses the hill above the visitor center and crosses Steep Creek twice before ending at the road by the parking lot. Salmon spawning is of special interest at Steep Creek—spawning sockeye (red) salmon from mid-July to mid-August and coho (silver) from mid-September to November. Males are recognized by large, fierce beaks and aggressive behavior. Fishing is not allowed nor advisable at this stage of decomposition. The USFS offers guided trips; ask for details at the visitor center.

East Glacier Trail takes off from the nature walk, about 200 yards above the visitor center. Climb the stairs around the center and turn left at the top. Turn left again across the hill toward the glacier. The climb is steep after crossing the A-J Waterfall (a water diversion built by miners several decades ago), and ascends in a series of zigzags. There are good views of the valley below and the Mendenhall Glacier terminus before the route follows Nugget Creek and joins the Nugget Creek trail (J15). Remains of a suspension footbridge and cabin may be found down by the river.

Where the paths meet, turn right and descend the Nugget Creek trail to rejoin the nature trail (at a covered display). Turn right again to return to the visitor center. Or turn left when reaching the nature trail to go to the parking lot by Steep Creek and the salmon spawning grounds (see map). Watch for a disintegrating wooden-and-wire flume shortly after joining the Nugget Creek Trail. Beware of ice on the path during winter. Crampons or creepers may be necessary for safe passage.

## J15
# NUGGET CREEK

**TIME:** 2.5 hours
**DISTANCE:** 3 miles to Vista Creek
**ELEVATION GAIN:** 1,200 feet
**RATING:** easy to moderate
**ACCESS:** East Glacier Trail (J14)
**TYPE:** deep valley, alpine bowls
**TRAIL CONDITION:** good
**MAP:** Juneau B-2

Ben Bollard, a placer miner, built this trail and for many years it was named after him. Nugget Creek, after which the trail is now named, discharges a torrent of water through a gorge into the east side of Mendenhall Glacier. A path threads through the valley in mixed stands of hemlock and spruce to a three-sided shelter at Vista Creek. It is possible to penetrate farther up the valley to Goat Creek and beyond, for views of the Nugget Spires and open alpine Upper Basin, but this involves a long session of bushwhacking. Hikers can also find ways onto Heintzelman Ridge, on the west side of Falls Creek, or up a gentle ridge that meets the trail at the western end of the Lower Basin.

See East Glacier Complex (J14) for the start of the Nugget Creek Trail; start from either end of the Mendenhall Glacier nature trail and

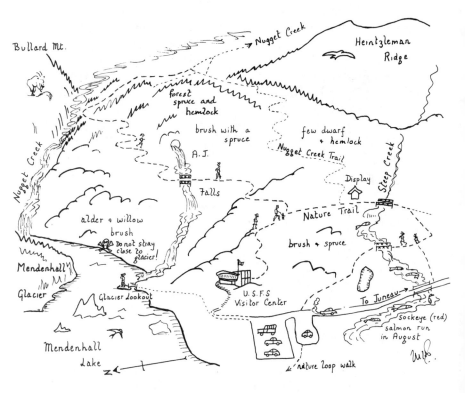

look for a well-used path leading up the hill from a covered display, about 0.25 mile from the USFS visitor center. This path climbs along slopes covered with thick alder and willow, and it offers occasional views of the glacier and Mendenhall Valley. Then it runs into ever-green trees, which are now gaining the ascendancy, and within 1 mile, it reaches the junction with the East Glacier Trail. Turn right for Nug-get Creek, or left to return to the nature trail and the visitor center.

From the junction it is about a 2-mile forest walk upriver to the Vista Creek shelter. From the shelter the trail deteriorates into brush, devil's club, alder, and nettles, and it is hard to follow as it climbs the lip of a deep gorge into the alpine meadows beyond.

*Derelict bridge, Nugget Creek*

# HEINTZELMAN RIDGE

**TIME:** 3.5 hours from visitor center
**DISTANCE:** 4.5 miles via Vista Creek
**ELEVATION GAIN:** 3,610 feet
**RATING:** strenuous
Route only

A steep, unmarked route on the west side of Fall Creek gives access to a flower-carpeted basin under two unnamed peaks on Heintzel-

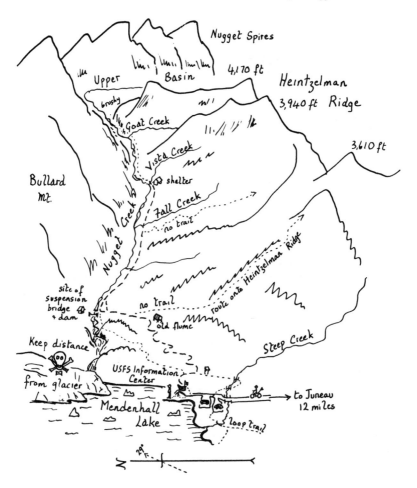

Nugget Spires

4,170 ft

Upper Basin

brushy

Goat Creek

Heintzelman
3,940 ft Ridge

3,610 ft

Vista Creek

shelter

Bullard mt.

Fall Creek

no trail

Nugget Creek

route onto Heintzelman Ridge

site of suspension bridge + dam

no trail

old flume

Keep distance

Steep Creek

from glacier

USFS Information Center

to Juneau
12 miles

Mendenhall Lake

loop trail

N

man Ridge, 3,610 feet and 3,940 feet above sea level. In clear weather the route to the ridge is strenuous, but not difficult. Be sure to take the Ten Essentials, especially foul-weather gear. Another route goes southeast up a gentle ridge leading onto "Peak 3610." This route starts just beyond a broken flume shortly before the Nugget Creek Trail reaches the East Glacier trail junction. The upper reaches of the ridge are open, and they give unbroken views of the Mendenhall Glacier and the mountains that ring the valley. In fall the sharply contrasting colors on a sunny day make this ridge walk hard to beat. Note: route-finding may be difficult and is only for those experienced in forest and mountain travel.

# J16
# THUNDER MOUNTAIN

**TIME:** 3 hours up
**DISTANCE:** 2.5 miles
**ELEVATION GAIN:** 2,950 feet
**RATING:** strenuous
**ACCESS:** bus to Mendenhall Valley
**TYPE:** forest, high alpine plateau
**TRAIL CONDITION:** poor
**MAP:** Juneau B-2
Route-finding abilities required

Thunder Mountain is the southernmost alpine peak on Heintzel-man Ridge, and it commands outstanding views of Auke Bay, the Mendenhall Valley, airport, glacier, town, and surrounding peaks. Later in the year, the upper basin is carpeted with flowers. But getting there is not easy. The trail is hard to find, and once found, hard to stay on. It is very wet especially on the east side at the beginning. Take along waterproof boots. This very important route needs adoption so that passable, legal access can be obtained onto the ridge. After all, most of the valley population seems to get up there sooner or later. It is the place to go for the views. The other access route from Switzer Creek is much better, and it is the recommended way.

From the East Mendenhall Valley Loop Road, turn right onto Trinity immediately after going under a pedestrian overpass (1 mile from the traffic lights). Turn left at the T junction, then immediately right onto Jennifer Drive to the end. From here, cross Jordan Creek; either wade or cross on a log. Turn left. Walk through deep, boggy marsh grass along what looks like a survey line, onto fairly good trail. Turn right past the remains of a log building. The path makes a couple of turns (a left, then a right), but with care it can be followed to a creek. Walk the creek briefly upstream and look for a trail on the right. Once found, it is fairly easy to follow up a subsidiary ridge onto the main southwest ridge of Thunder Mountain. Mark the spot where this route merges with the others on the ridge, for the return; and be aware of false trails, especially those leading downslope. It is very easy to miss the trail on the return. The tendency is to descend too early where the slopes become steep and forests of devil's club predominate. Do not try to descend farther. Climb back to the ridge to the original route.

Above 1,500 feet the forest ridge walk becomes very pleasant and

*Mendenhall Glacier from Thunder Mountain*

gives glimpses of the summit through thinning trees. On attaining
open ridge, the route climbs steeply to the summit through grass and
flower meadows. Travelers are advised not to use this route as access
onto the other peaks of Heintzelman Ridge. Ridge gendarmes force
one onto a short, but dangerously steep traverse under the main ridge.

Most townsfolk start at the south end of Malissa Drive, but this
crosses private land and permission must be obtained before venturing across.

## SWITZER CREEK ACCESS ROUTE

**TIME:** 2.5 hours
**DISTANCE:** 2 miles
**ELEVATION GAIN:** same
**ACCESS:** city bus to Department of Transportation, 6 miles northwest
   of Juneau
   Drive 6 miles north of town, to the first right turn past the Lemon

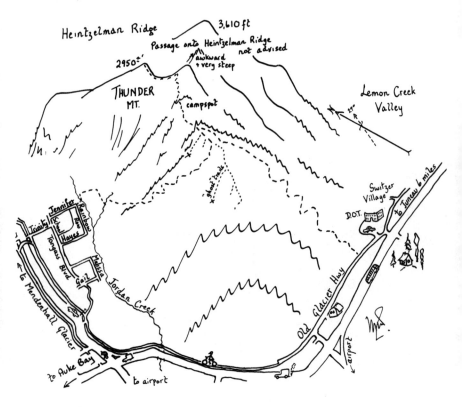

Creek traffic lights. Immediately turn left, then right into the Department of Transportation parking lot. Walk north along the old Glacier Highway about 400 yards to the signed trailhead. This route climbs steeply in places in the ridge, where it joins the other trail. The junction is marked and is easy to recognize for the return. On the way up, when emerging into muskeg, turn right almost immediately. Do not follow the opening to its logical end. This route meets the well-traveled Valley trail at about 1,800 feet elevation.

# J17
# WEST GLACIER AND MOUNT MCGINNIS

**TIME:** 2.5 hours
**DISTANCE:** 3 miles
**ELEVATION GAIN:** 1,300 feet
**RATING:** moderate
**ACCESS:** West Mendenhall Lake Campgrounds, 3.5 miles from Auke Bay
**TYPE:** glacial overlook
**TRAIL CONDITION:** good
**MAP:** Juneau B-2

The West Mendenhall Glacier Trail is a revelation to those who have never seen a glacier firsthand. This is one of the few places where the casual hiker can gain entry into the mountaineer's mystical world

*Mendenhall Glacier from West Glacier Trail*

*Canadian dogwood*

without the skills and trappings of the rock and ice climber. Mount McGinnis is a long walk, but it is a walk, nonetheless, when winter snows are gone, and it offers a high-angle view of the same world, with the ice cap, Nugget Spires, and Mendenhall Towers thrown in. This trail is used by many for access onto the Mendenhall Glacier above the icefall and to climb local surrounding peaks. Only those experienced in glacier travel should venture onto the ice. This trail is administered by the USFS.

Drive to the Auke Bay boat harbor, 11.4 miles from town, and take the Mendenhall Back Loop Road, which turns right off the main road opposite the harbor. After 2.4 miles, turn left onto a dirt road posted to Mendenhall Lake Campgrounds, then keep right at the Y junction with Montana Creek Road (0.3 mile). Go past the camp-

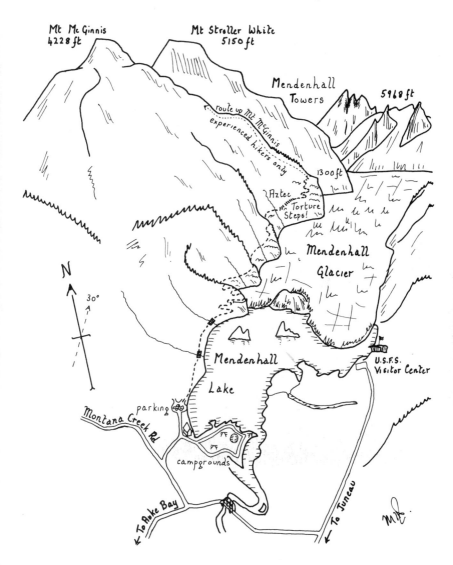

grounds to the end of the dirt road, to a parking area and trailhead, 1
mile from the Back Loop road.

The first mile is a flat walk by the lake through alder, willow, cottonwood, and small spruce and across several streams. Then the path
switchbacks steeply up a bluff onto rock slabs to a superb view of the

Mendenhall Glacier. From here it traverses the lower slopes of Mount McGinnis, crossing many streams and ascending steeply in places. Toward the end, the route is more difficult to follow over small rock bluffs, keep left and upward when in doubt.

Finally, gain a large rock platform above the first icefall (an abrupt drop in levels characterized by a jumbled mass of broken ice). The glacier widens above, forming a "bay" under the lower, abrupt slopes of Mount Stroller White, and then surrounds the rock promontory on three sides. Mountains rise almost sheer on all sides. Only those with good route-finding abilities and some experience in mountain travel should go on.

# MOUNT McGINNIS

**TIME:** 4–5 hours
**DISTANCE:** 4.5 miles
**ELEVATION GAIN:** 4,228 feet
**RATING:** strenuous
Primitive route

A flagged route marks the way onto Mount McGinnis; it is a little hard to find at the beginning. Once clear of the brush and rock, the route is easier to follow as it goes northwest across a small stream onto the east ridge of the mountain. The path breaks out of trees at about 2,300 feet into a tarn-sprinkled area, with some gorgeous meadows. Please do not tramp across the large one, but stay high and to the right to avoid damage to the delicate plant ecosystem. Note where the trail emerges from the trees, for the return. From here it is an easy, but long slog to the summit across alpine meadows. The views of the glacier at one's feet and distant Fairweather Range west of Glacier Bay make the day an unforgettable experience. An ice ax is needed for winter and early spring travel.

# J18

# AUKE NU AND SPAULDING MEADOWS SKI CIRCUIT

## AUKE NU TRAIL

**TIME:** 2.5 hours
**DISTANCE:** 3 miles
**ELEVATION GAIN:** 1,550 feet
**RATING:** moderate
**ACCESS:** Auke Bay, 11.5 miles from Juneau
**TYPE:** mountain meadowland
**TRAIL CONDITION:** good
**MAPS:** Juneau B-2 and B-3
Overnight cabin

Two trails give access to the open meadows on the gradual, sloping high ground north of Auke Bay. Auke Nu, the westward trail, is mainly boardwalk. It climbs to the John Muir cabin on high ground overlooking the Peterson Lake drainage, Auke Bay, and Mendenhall Flats. In winter, the meadows to the east are used extensively by skiers. Many stay overnight at the cabin, then ski on high ground to pick up the end of the Spaulding Trail, and descend from there. Allow 6 hours for the circuit. Some skiers also pick their own way from the cabin, north-northwest cross-country to Peterson Lake. Day use of the cabin is allowed without reservation or fee, but overnight use must be prearranged with the USFS. These trails are administered by the USFS.

A small parking place is found on the right side of the main highway, 0.2 mile beyond the Auke Bay post office. Do not cross Waydelich Creek. The trail starts as a corduroy road that climbs gently uphill and makes a sharp turn to cross a stream ditch. After the first mile, shortly before emerging into the first open muskeg, the trail divides. Turn left to go to John Muir cabin.

Shortly after the division, Auke Nu Trail crosses Waydelich Creek running through a small ravine. The boardwalk trail then climbs steadily through spruce, hemlock, and small pine in semi-open country. It briefly follows the lip of a gorge above Auke Nu Creek. Toward the top, the way is boggy. The cabin sits on high ground in open, gently sloping country. Auke Mountain can be seen to the west. The trail is marked with blue diamonds, which help skiers locate the route when it is covered with snow.

To make a loop, go northwest and stay on high ground over a wooded hill for about 1.5 miles. The Spaulding Trail is picked up beyond a small ridge. Look for tracks and diamond-shaped markers on the trees. Use a map and compass to help find the way.

## SPAULDING MEADOWS

**TIME:** 2.5 hours
**DISTANCE:** 3 miles
**ELEVATION GAIN:** 1,700 feet
**TRAIL CONDITION:** poor
Allow 6 hours for Auke-Nu–Spaulding Meadows circuit ski route

*Gastineau Channel from Spaulding Meadows*

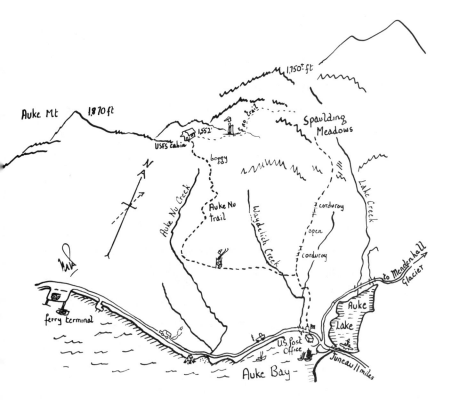

Spaulding Trail follows a corduroy mining road on the east side of Waydelich Creek to some abandoned claims close to a large stretch of open meadows above Lake Creek.

Keep going straight at the trail division to reach Spaulding Meadows on the miner's road. The old trail goes gently uphill through trees, then muskeg where views are obtained of Auke Bay. Look back to remember where the trail emerges from the trees for the return. It follows a stream system and runs through two small openings, the second containing a derelict log cabin, before it emerges into high meadows. Although there is enough traffic now to make the tread visible, watch for colored markers on the return to locate the trail end.

This trail has wicked bog holes in summer, so wear waterproof boots. However, the meadows are covered with white orchis and active insectivorous plants such as sundew and butterwort or bog violet. In late summer they are white with Alaska bog cotton. Far glimpses of tidal water are visible, and the area is dominated by shapely peaks to the northwest.

*Peterson Mill tramway*

# J19
# PETERSON LAKE

**TIME:** 2 hours
**DISTANCE:** 4.3 miles
**ELEVATION GAIN:** 750 feet
**RATING:** easy to moderate
**ACCESS:** 22 miles north of Juneau
**TYPE:** historical, forest, fishing
**TRAIL CONDITION:** excellent
**MAP:** Juneau B-3
Overnight cabin

John Peterson staked a claim in 1899 and called it Cheechako Creek. At first he used a trail to haul in supplies from Tee Harbor. Later he built a tramway from the beach to his three-stamp mill. The tramway can be seen today, especially in the lower elevations. Steelhead is found below the falls in Peterson Creek, and rainbow and Dolly Varden trout are fished from the lake. (Winter fishing is great fun!) The USFS John Peterson Family Cabin, built by local volunteers, is located on a pleasant opening on the southwestern lakeshore. It is a link in a cross-country ski trek from Auke Bay and John Muir cabin (see J18). However, this is strictly map and compass cross-country orienteering; there is no marked route between cabins. Peterson Lake Trail and cabin are administered by the USFS. Be sure to register with the USFS for an overnight stay.

Peterson Lake trail is partially boardwalk. It starts near to milepost 24 on Glacier Highway, immediately south of Peterson Creek. The trail gradually ascends through stands of spruce and western hemlock, closely following the creek upstream. Within about 15 minutes, a steep primitive spur trail drops into the gorge to a fishing hole directly below some falls. The main route then emerges into wet, but pretty, meadows, where the disintegrating tram route is plainly seen. Note the dogwood clusters growing between the planks. Here the Peterson Lake trail leaves the old tramway, veering to the right and staying on the west bank of Peterson Creek to the lake. By following the tramway farther, persistent history buffs, who don't mind bushwhacking, may find the old mining encampment on the other side of Peterson Creek, 0.5 mile east of Peterson Lake.

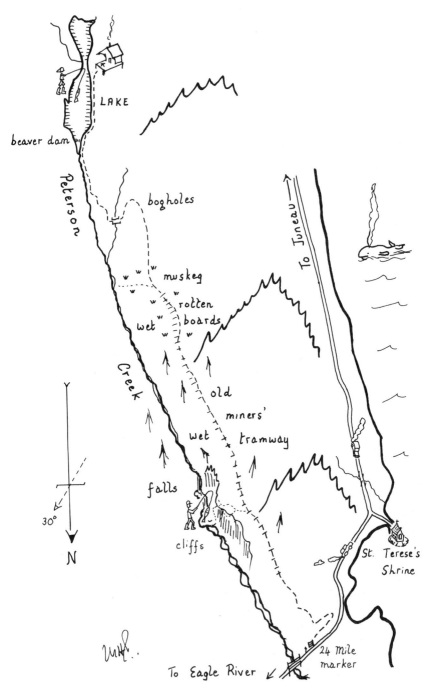

LAKE

beaver dam

Peterson

bogholes

muskeg

rotten
boards

wet

Creek

old

miners'

wet tramway

falls

30°

N

cliffs

To Juneau

St. Terese's
Shrine

24 Mile
marker

To Eagle River

# J20
# MONTANA CREEK

**TIME:** 6 hours
**DISTANCE:** 12.3 miles
**ELEVATION GAIN:** 800 ± feet
**RATING:** moderate to strenuous
**ACCESS:** Windfall Lake Trail (J21) or Montana Creek Road
**TYPE:** forest, meadows, fishing at extremities
**TRAIL CONDITION:** poor
**MAPS:** Juneau B-2, B-3, and C-3

Montana Creek Trail connects Windfall Lake (J21) and Montana Creek systems over a low pass. For the entire route, be sure to have a car at each end of the trip. It can be a summer walk through forests and meadows, or a winter ski run over the northern half when the rivers are not frozen, or the entire route in cold winters. It is also possible for ambitious cross-country skiers, armed with map and compass plus knowledge of local terrain, to make connections with the Spaulding trail or the John Muir cabin (see J18).

Montana Creek has good fishing for salmon and Dolly Varden and cutthroat trout. Bears have a reputation for being common along Montana Creek, and although sightings are fairly rare, be sure to have the large noisy bear bells along just in case!

Until the USFS reroutes the trail around the slide areas, it is advisable to start from Montana Creek. Take the Mendenhall Back Loop Road from Auke Bay, 2.4 miles towards the Mendenhall Glacier. Turn left onto Montana Creek Road (posted "USFS campgrounds"). Bear left at a Y junction and go to the end of the road, 3.6 miles. The trail starts here and follows Montana Creek upstream.

The southward route starts from the Windfall Lake trail (J21). Walk for about an hour (2.8 miles) on good trail. Look for a turn to the left, at the end of some planking (shortly before reaching the last of the large beaver ponds and a 100-foot hill that lies just north of Windfall Lake). This division is only about 10 to 15 minutes from the lake.

The path from the north end runs along the east side of Windfall Lake (which is visible) to open meadows at the far end, and some campsites close to the south end of the lake. The trail is very wet and runs through groves of devil's club. About 1 mile from the lake, the path seems to disappear across a stream, but in fact, it turns left up the streambed for a few yards before crossing over. After 2 miles, the trail fords Windfall Creek and turns sharply left following the right bank of the creek upstream.

The path then climbs steadily above Windfall Creek and some

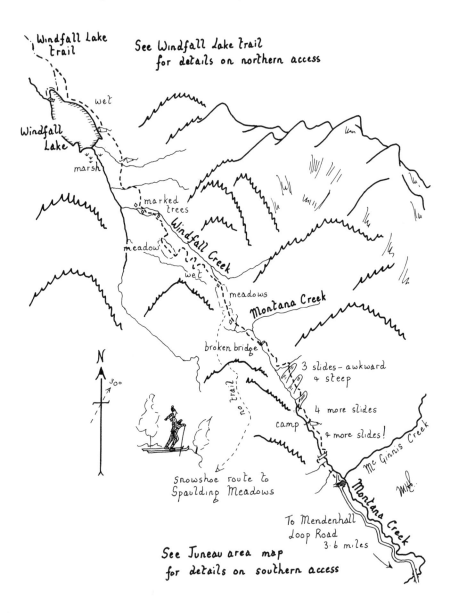

pretty waterfalls and eventually emerges from trees into a small meadow. At the far end, it turns left once more and switchbacks upward through pleasant forest groves with streams on both sides, until it finally emerges into a series of large open meadows. The route becomes boggy again, and the path continues its general southeasterly course. An unnamed ridge and the striking peaks above Herbert and Eagle glaciers dominate the northeast skyline. The meadows form the watershed of the Windfall and Montana Creek drainages, and from here the route descends through forests. It crosses a tributary of Montana Creek and, shortly afterward, the main stream by a broken bridge. Take care; the bridge is slippery. Then it ends in a series of slides over the swiftly flowing river, one of which is very unstable and exposed to a fall into the river. The USFS is considering rerouting the trail above the slide area. From here the route is easy going to the road.

# J21
# WINDFALL LAKE

**TIME:** 1.5 hours
**DISTANCE:** 3.5 miles
**ELEVATION GAIN:** 80 feet
**RATING:** easy
**ACCESS:** car, milepost 27 north of Juneau
**TYPE:** forest, fishing, beaver ponds
**TRAIL CONDITION:** good
**MAPS:** Juneau B-3 and C-3

Despite the trail's good condition, take waterproof boots along for the unexpected bottomless hole and to allow a walk around the lake. Also take a fishing pole, as the lake contains Dolly Varden and cutthroat trout. Many people ski the trail in winter and fish through the ice. The route follows Herbert River closely for about 1.5 miles, offering upriver views of the ragged, striking peaks above Herbert Glacier; it then penetrates a deep forest of old moss-covered trees and mature devil's club.

Drive north of Juneau, past Auke Bay, to the Herbert River, shortly after the milepost 27, 25.7 miles northwest of Juneau. Turn right on a dirt road, about 200 yards before crossing the river, and

drive to its end. The trail starts on the right side of the parking area, and travels upriver to a swift-flowing stream (a splintered half of the Herbert River) where dwarf spruce and lichen predominate. The stream, which is recrossed, is a raging torrent in spring and could be a danger to anyone who falls in. The bridges are adequate, but keep children close by.

As soon as the path leaves the river, it goes into beaver pond country. Many years ago, a trail went off from here to Herbert Glacier, but after perennial flooding by beavers, it was abandoned. The present Windfall Lake trail passes over and by many ponds before it reaches the lake. Shortly after the junction with Montana Creek Trail, the trail turns right to avoid a 100-foot hill, and it takes 10 to 15 minutes to reach the lake.

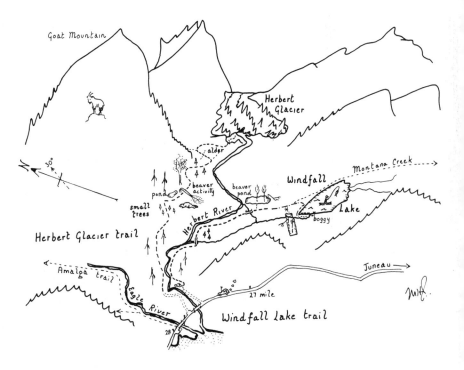

*On the trail to Windfall Lake*

# J22
# HERBERT GLACIER

**TIME:** 2.5 hours
**DISTANCE:** 4.7 miles
**ELEVATION GAIN:** 350 ± feet
**RATING:** moderate
**ACCESS:** 26 miles northwest of Juneau
**TYPE:** flat valley, mature forests
**TRAIL CONDITION:** good to fair
**MAP:** Juneau C-3

This beautiful walk has gained about 600 yards in the past two decades. The glacier has receded and alders have replaced once bare terrain. People ski here in the winter, and if it is cold enough, they ignore the trail and follow the frozen river. Unfortunately, this valley is threatened by future mining activity, including road building. This will have a devastating effect on the wildness and pristine beauty of the area. This trail is administered by the USFS.

Drive the highway 26 miles north from Juneau and cross the Herbert River. The parking area and trail are on the right, 0.5 mile beyond the 27 miles marker. The route starts out as a road for the first mile or so in mature spruce and hemlock forests. As it enters a young uniform hemlock forest carpeted with moss, it becomes a footpath and partial boardwalk. After about 2 miles the path provides skyline views of Goat Mountain straight ahead—the original destination of this trail. Here the trees are small, and the ground covered with lichens and mosses. About halfway, pass an active beaver pond with totemlike carvings. Look for trees still standing after being half chewed and scored with tooth marks. Sometimes the travels of a tree felled by the beavers are written in the mud of their trail or on the pool bank.

Travelers beware: this trail is easily lost in hard spring snow, and the return route to the road may be difficult to find.

The route skirts the base of Goat Mountain on the north side of the valley and emerges onto terminal moraine after going through tall alder and willow and more lovely moss- and lichen-covered ground. The view of the glacier is stunning. It has a waterfall on both sides and can be approached over bare ground. Do not venture onto the ice without an ice ax, rope, and some knowledge of how to use them.

# J23
# AMALGA-EAGLE GLACIER

**TIME:** 3.5 hours
**DISTANCE:** 5.5 miles
**ELEVATION GAIN:** 1,200 feet round trip
**RATING:** moderate to strenuous
**ACCESS:** milepost 28 north of Juneau
**TYPE:** forest, valley, beaver ponds, historical
**TRAIL CONDITION:** good first 1.5 miles
**MAP:** Juneau C-3

In the early 1900s, this route was a horse tramway, from the beach to the Amalga Mine, about 1 mile west of Eagle Glacier. The mine settlement was large enough to warrant a post office, and a wharf

*Eagle River*

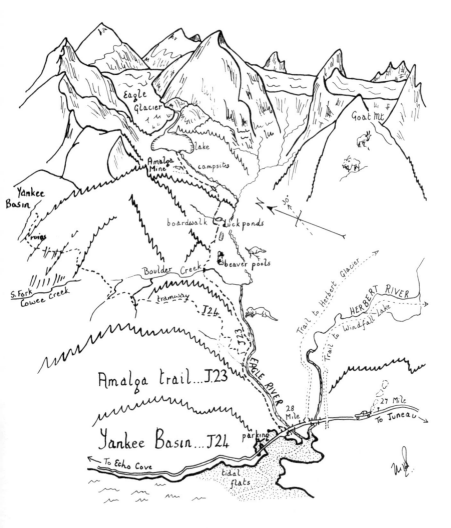

and warehouse existed on the beach. Now it is a long interesting walk to a viewpoint of the glacier. Little evidence remains of mine buildings or bunkhouses at the Amalga site. Unfortunately, frequent beaver-inspired floodings necessitated changing the route up the hillside in three places. The hills are steep, hard on knees, and practically unskiable, and they add many hundreds of feet of climbing to get to the glacier. When snow conditions are good and the river frozen over, many people ski up the river to the beaver ponds. The altitude at trail end is 200 feet.

Drive the highway 26.5 miles north of Juneau. Immediately after crossing Eagle River (close to the milepost 28) park on the left side of the road. The trail follows the river upstream, and within 1 mile, it meets the Yankee Basin Trail (J24). A few more minutes of riverbank walking and the trail begins to climb, following the western slope. Then it drops to a meadow and some beaver ponds, where it departs the old trail and climbs again to cross Boulder Creek.

A campsite by a stream is located about half a mile back from the present end of trail. The walk finishes at a lake at the base of the glacier, which can be seen about a mile away. The USFS plans to extend the trail through the heavy shoreline brush to give access to the glacier.

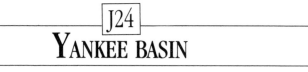

# J24
# YANKEE BASIN

**TIME:** 4 hours
**DISTANCE:** 5.2 miles
**ELEVATION GAIN:** 1,700 feet round trip
**RATING:** moderate to strenuous
**ACCESS:** Amalga-Eagle Glacier trail (J23)
**TYPE:** historical, forest
**TRAIL CONDITION:** fair
**MAP:** C-3

This trail follows a tramway on a gentle gradient to a high, secluded basin at the headwaters of the South Fork of Cowee Creek. Distant views of Echo Cove, Bridget Point, and Chilkats across Lynn Canal are obtained on a hill traverse to Yankee Basin. A route has been brushed as far as a waterfall at the head of the valley on the 1,200-foot contour, several hundred feet below the mine workings. A mine shaft and the remains of a cabin are visible at the current trail end, and the Forest Service plans to brush onto the ridge almost a mile farther. Fresh bear sign and the bears themselves (black, brown or both) are frequently seen along this route, especially where it crosses the head of Boulder Creek and runs along the sidehill above the South Fork of Cowee Creek. There are several small slides on the steep slopes toward the end.

Take Amalga-Eagle Glacier trail (J23) at least 1 mile along Eagle River to a junction. Take the left turn, which climbs about 700 feet through many boggy patches, to the wooden tramway. Turn right. (A sign here suggests the tramway as an alternate way to the road, but hikers are advised to ignore this on the way down. The tramway is hard to follow and has been obliterated by slides.) The old wagon road climbs steadily through forests, and one can see evidence of selective logging, probably during the building of the tramway and the mine buildings. Huge trees were felled, after notches were cut in the trunk for a sawing platform. The tramway is beginning to slide sideways in places, so be careful when the boards are wet. It crosses a couple of major side streams before emerging into muskeg. Snow-covered peaks above Eagle Glacier are just visible about halfway along the trail.

At the head of Boulder Creek, the country opens into meadows, with large open muskeg patches on the slopes to the west. Take care to follow the route across the watershed, and traverse the west slope of the South Fork, maintaining height. From here, enjoy a good view of points north. Watch for bear sign and make noise. The tramway, still visible in places, traverses the hill at about 1,500-feet elevation, then it descends gradually to a stream crossing in Yankee Basin. Slippage occurs at places, making passage awkward, but hikers are rewarded with good views of the basin and ridge above.

# POINT BRIDGET AND BRIDGET COVE

**TIME:** 3.5 hours to Point Bridget
**DISTANCE:** 4.1 miles
**ELEVATION GAIN:** 200 ± feet
**RATING:** moderate
**ACCESS:** milepost 38 north of Juneau
**TYPE:** beach, river meadow
**TRAIL CONDITION:** poor at present, upgrading is planned
**MAP:** Juneau C-3
Check tides for beach walks

This new, raw trail in a state park still needs a lot of work. It travels through a biologically diverse area, including old-growth forest, muskegs, salt marshes, beaches, beaver ponds, a lake, and a

*Chilkat Mountains from North Bridget Cove*

lovely stand of cedars. The route leads to the northern and western-most point west of Echo Cove, and on its way it passes large estuarine meadows, which are carpeted with flowers in early June and July. Almost 3 miles from the road, another trail, unofficially named "Cedar Lake," runs south past a small lake to tidewater at the north end of Bridget Cove. A third alternative is a 30-minute walk to Bridget Cove. Be sure to have tide tables handy for beach walking. The state plans to

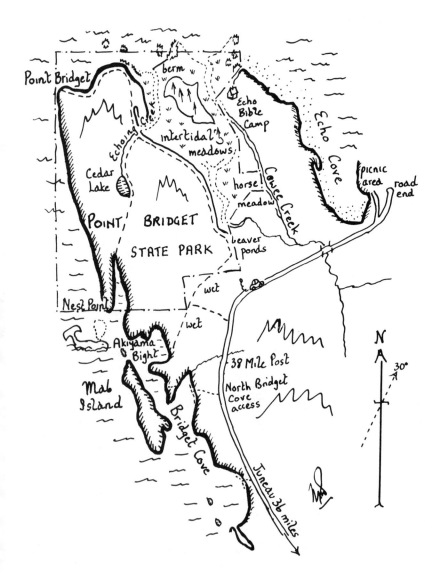

put in boardwalk at the beginning and to replace the beaver dam with a bridge.

Drive to a turn in the road just beyond milepost 38 (2.7 miles from the road end at Echo Cove). A path leads into the trees by an information board, climbs over a small hill, and drops to the old trail. Turn left for the beach, turn right for Point Bridget. The trail to the right is very wet, and it drops into a beaver swamp. Cross over the beaver dam, and circle left to follow the hillside. The trail parallels the Cowee Creek meadows just inside the forest. For variety, venture out onto the meadows to view myriad wildflowers. Horses from a local ranch may be seen in the meadows. The trail can be rejoined anywhere along here without difficulty.

The route crosses the Cedar Lake outflow (a tiny stream) and continues north, then west along the shore, 1.2 miles to Point Bridget. There is good camping and running water east of the point.

## BRIDGET COVE VIA CEDAR LAKE

**TIME:** 2.5 hours
**DISTANCE:** 5 miles
**ELEVATION GAIN:** 600 feet

Just before Cedar Lake outflow, almost 3 miles from the road, turn left at a junction (presently unmarked) and travel uphill to Cedar Lake, so named by locals because of an outstanding stand of cedar trees along its shore. Hikers can continue south past the lake on a fairly well-defined trail for about a mile to a secluded beach complete with eagle's nest. From here a path of sorts returns along beach bluffs to North Bridge Cove and the beach access trails from the road.

## BRIDGET COVE BY SHORT ROUTE

**TIME:** 30 minutes
**DISTANCE:** 1 mile

Turn left at the first T junction after leaving the road, and follow an old public access trail to the beach. Explore the beach to the north or to the south; look for routes across the headlands. Folks going south may rejoin the road at the North Bridget Cove beach access. Those going north may link up with the Bridget Point system once more.

# SITKA

IN pre-Russian times Sitka was Shee-Atika, a Kiksadi clan village of the Tlingit nation. After a fierce battle in 1804, the Russians drove the Native Alaskans off the land and named the new town and fortifications Novo Arkhangelsk "New Archangel," which in time became the capital of Russian America. Modern Sitka was born after the sale of Alaska to the United States (for 7.2 million dollars) in 1867. The event is celebrated annually on October 18. Today Sitka retains its charm as a historic city. A Russian Orthodox church of classic beauty and elegance, restored after being burned to the ground in 1966, lends a Byzantine flavor to the city. The Bishop's House, home of Father Ivan Veniaminov for many years, is one of the last remaining examples of nineteenth-century Russian colonial architecture. Also, a reconstructed blockhouse indicates the fortifications the Russians used during their subsequent uneasy truce with the Kiksadi clan.

Sitka is situated in a natural harbor on the west coast of Baranof Island. Pacific Ocean swells are broken by a chain of forested islands that protects the entrance to Sitka Harbor. Shapely spires rise 3,000 to 4,000 feet almost immediately from the outskirts of town and continue around the bay in a sweep of sharp alpine peaks. A dormant volcano, Mount Edgecumbe, stands guard to seaward.

Access through the front door is by jet onto a runway facing Sitka. The Alaska State ferry threads its way through a maze of sea passages to gain sheltered and scenic access into Starrigavan Bay (Russian for "Old Harbor"), 7 miles north of town, close to the end of Halibut Point Road.

A USFS campground is available for motor campers and tent campers almost 1 mile north of the ferry terminal, and an unimproved campground is found at Sawmill Creek, close to the pulp mill at the east end of the road system (see Beaver Lake St6). The city of Sitka has recreational vehicle parking at Sealing Cove, across the bridge on Japonski Island. Walk around Sitka to see Castle Hill, where the Russian-American transfer took place, and go by Crescent Harbor to Sheldon Jackson College, to see the museum and the Alaska Raptor Rehabilitation Center. Here injured bald eagles are exercised along a tethered flight line, in preparation for release into the wild. Bicycling the road both ways is very enjoyable. Going north, many pullouts pro-

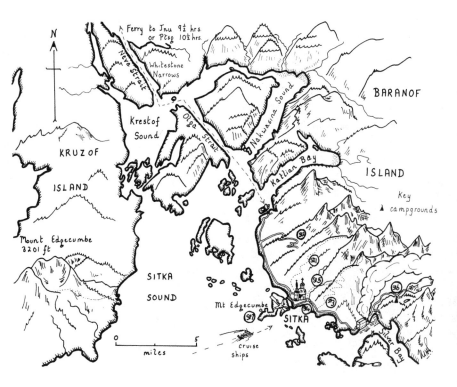

vide views of the seascape and birdlife. A state recreation area at Halibut Point has covered picnic sites, forest trails for young and old, and sites for intertidal exploration. Beyond the ferry terminal is the site of Old Sitka, where the Russians first settled in 1799. They suffered an initial defeat at the hands of the Kiksadi Tlingits in 1802.

Trails not formally described are: Thimbleberry Lake, 3.5 miles on Sawmill Creek Road (a half mile long, in good condition, and well marked); the Wraparound Trail (Cross Trail), from Gavan Hill Trail west to Charteris Street (brush has been cleared back and follows jeep trails); and Mount Edgecumbe, 3,201 feet high on Kruzof Island. The latter requires boat access to a beach exposed to heavy swells, and it can be approached only during quiet weather intervals. The USFS, Sitka Ranger District, maintains a cabin on the beach at Fred's Creek, 10 miles west of Sitka.

Suggested topographic maps are: Sitka A-4 and A-5 (plus A-6 for Mount Edgecumbe). Mileages to trailheads are taken from the south end of Swan Lake.

*Sitka Sound from Gavan Hill*

## St1
# GAVAN HILL

**TIME:** 3 hours
**DISTANCE:** 3 miles
**ELEVATION GAIN:** 2,700 ± feet
**RATING:** strenuous
**ACCESS:** foot from town
**TYPE:** wooded hillside, alpine
**TRAIL CONDITION:** good
**MAPS:** Sitka A-4 and A-5

Gavan Hill is a dominant feature of the northern skyline and offers extensive views of Sitka, Sitka Sound, and the sugarloaf Sister peaks inland. This well-defined trail starts from the north end of downtown

Sitka and climbs onto the ridge in a series of switchbacks. An awkward climb up rock and mountain hemlock gives access to the first and most magnificent viewpoint at approximately 2,500 feet. From here the hiker can range over the next peak or onto the bumpy ridge between Gavan Hill and Harbor Mountain. The USFS is working on a trail to connect this high ground to the Harbor Mountain road head. Cross-country hikers are warned to keep an eye on the weather and take compass bearings as they go. Opaque, dank clouds can descend swiftly, and it is easy to get lost. Water is scarce on the summit; one pool of doubtful quality exists on high ground during dry summers. Otherwise, stream trickles are found close to a semi-viewpoint about halfway to the ridge. Campers should also take cooking stoves since wood is scarce on the ridge.

From the center of town, find the Centennial Building, then Crescent Harbor (a small boat harbor to the east). Turn left up Baranof Street past a grade school. Cross over Sawmill Creek Road and Merrill Road and walk to the last house on the right. Look for a trail immediately beyond the house and shortly before reaching the city cemetery. The ground is wet at the start, but the trail is on boardwalk much of

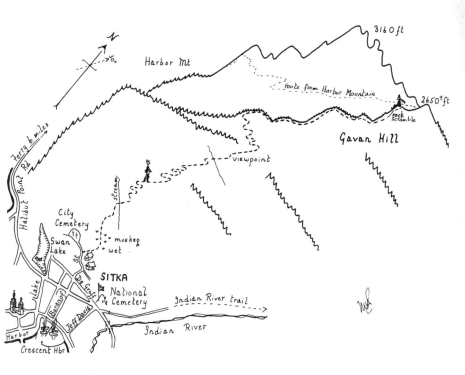

the way to the beginning of the climb. The route climbs steadily through groves of huge Sitka spruce and hemlock. It crosses a stream gully then climbs more earnestly through a series of switchbacks until, after about 1.5 hours of walking, a resting point is reached with views onto Indian River. The trail climbs more steeply in a series of short zig-zags from here to the ridge. A flat area large enough for a medium-sized tent is found as soon as the ridge is reached.

Continue northeast, climbing gently through diminishing trees to a fragile meadow and the first viewpoint of the Sisters. A short steep climb of approximately 200 feet gives access to the first peak. Be sure to stay on the ridge to avoid steep rocks on the left (west). The second, higher peak allows one to see the headwaters of the north fork of the Indian River, and it gives extensive views of a massive jumble of ice-hung peaks towards the interior of Baranof Island. Continue north to a 2,505-foot hill (marked on the topographic map) to link with the Harbor Mountain Route (St 2).

# St2
# HARBOR MOUNTAIN

**TIME:** 1.5 hours
**DISTANCE:** 1.4 miles
**ELEVATION GAIN:** 1,200 feet round trip
**RATING:** moderate, traverse is strenuous
**ACCESS:** Harbor Mountain road, 4.1 miles from Halibut Point Road
**TYPE:** semi-alpine and alpine
**TRAIL CONDITION:** good on ridge, cross-country to Gavan Hill
**MAPS:** Sitka A-4 and A-5

A narrow, winding dirt road built during World War II climbs 5 miles to a shoulder of Harbor Mountain. The road is steep and has several S bends, so do not be tempted to drive with RVs or trailers. Half a mile from the road end, at 2,000 feet, there is a covered picnic area with picnic tables scattered over the semi-open alp. The picnic area is administered by the USFS and gives extensive views of Sitka Sound and surrounding islands. From the end of the road, a partial boardwalk leads onto the ridge running east-northeast towards Harbor Mountain. A spur trail turns right (west) to the 2,370-foot hill directly above the

*Starrigavan Bay and Nakwasina Sound from Harbor Mountain*

road. Ruins of World War II fortifications are hard to find on top, but look for holes in the ground. The views of Sitka from here are superb.

Walk along the ridge for good views of Harbor Mountain, Olga Strait, the ferry terminal, surrounding islands, and the Pacific.

## GAVAN HILL TRAVERSE

**TIME:** 4.5 hours to Sitka
**DISTANCE:** 6 miles
**ELEVATION GAIN:** 1,300 feet
**RATING:** strenuous

A well-defined trail climbs over a ridge hump and traverses a steep shoulder of Harbor Mountain, then descends towards the Gavan

Hill Ridge. The USFS plans to complete the trail to the ridge so that people may walk from here to town by the Gavan Hill trail (see St1). At present it is not too difficult to pick the way across the mountain slope. Be sure to have a map and compass before committing to this route. Weather changes are sudden.

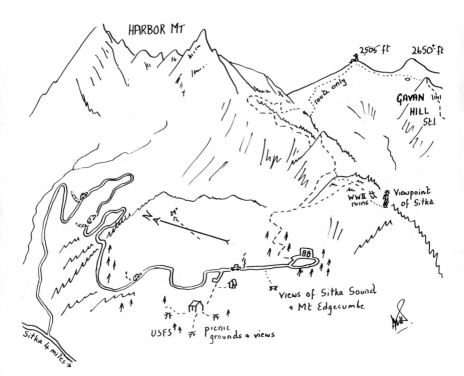

# Mount Verstovia

**TIME:** 2.5 hours to viewpoint
**DISTANCE:** 3 miles
**ELEVATION GAIN:** 2,550 feet
**RATING:** strenuous
**ACCESS:** 2 miles southeast of Sitka
**TYPE:** forest, alpine
**TRAIL CONDITION:** poor
**MAP:** Sitka A-4

Mount Verstovia, a shapely, pointed peak, dominates Sitka to the east. Its commanding position gives the hiker uninterrupted views of Sitka, the scattering of surf-washed islands guarding Sitka Harbor, and open Pacific Ocean. A Russian *verst* equals a mile, and the Russians considered this peak to be one verst high, hence the name Mount Verstovia. The lower slopes of the mountain were logged by the Russians more than a century ago, and the even-age regrowth shows a

*Harbor Mountain from Mount Verstovia*

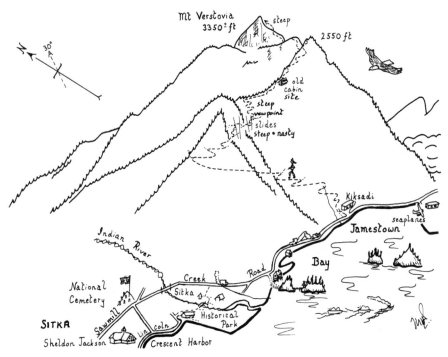

thick understory. Some Russian charcoal pits were located about 0.25 mile from the trailhead. Unfortunately, the trail is in poor shape and is easily lost in places because of "ghost trails" on the turns. One point is especially steep with an awkward scramble. Until maintenance work can be done, it is not recommended for casual visitors to Sitka. The viewpoint will be sufficient for most people, since the climb to the final summit is steep and exposed and should not be attempted in snow without an ice ax. Daytime parking is allowed at the Kiksadi Club, and hikers may use their telephone in emergencies.

Take Sawmill Creek Road, the major shoreline road east of town, to the Kiksadi Club. Those walking the full distance from town may prefer to walk around Crescent Harbor and through the Sitka National Historical Park (see St4). The trail starts on the west side of the Kiksadi Club and climbs on boardwalk for the first few yards. It ascends through brush by a low-level view of Sitka, then goes more steeply in a series of zigzags. Beware of the ghost trails, which continue on a few yards after the true trail has turned the corner. The route is steep above an old slide, and there is an awkward climb by a broken ladder to a worthwhile view of Mount Edgecumbe. (Be sure to zigzag. Ghost trails mislead here too.) A compassionate soul has placed a log bench at this viewpoint, almost at the halfway point. The last 500 feet of climbing before the final ridge is steep with diminishing switchbacks, which are largely ignored and contribute to the destruction of the trail. From there the climb is moderate up the ridge through smaller western and mountain hemlock trees. From the high viewpoint, the city of Sitka lies in miniature at the base of the ridge.

## SUMMIT ROUTE

**TIME:** 4 hours
**DISTANCE:** 4 miles
**ELEVATION GAIN:** 3,650 feet

A narrower footpath descends from the viewpoint about 300 feet to a saddle between the viewpoint and the Mount Verstovia summit, 3,350± feet elevation (often mistaken for Arrowhead Peak). This sheer-walled, triangular peak towers 1,000 feet over the saddle. Climbers and experienced hikers may attempt the final summit by following the ridge above the saddle, then traversing to steep grass slopes on the right of the final rock scarp. Be careful from here. One slip could land a person at the front door of the pulp mill 3,000 feet below. The views from the summit are lofty indeed. Below are the somber depths of Silver Bay and the broken coastline of Sitka Sound. To the east a wicked-looking ridge makes a drunken walk to the Arrowhead Peak marked on the topographic map. Behind this rise the shapely Sisters and a tumbled mass of mountains and ice fields forming the backbone of Baranof Island.

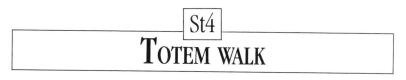

# St4
# TOTEM WALK

**TIME:** 40 minutes to 1 hour
**DISTANCE:** 1 mile
**ELEVATION GAIN:** none
**RATING:** easy
**ACCESS:** 1 mile east of town
**TYPE:** historical, shoreline
**TRAIL CONDITION:** excellent

The tiny Sitka National Historical Park (administered by the NPS) on the eastern end of Crescent Bay takes up the half mile of beach to Indian River. It was here that the Tlingit natives of the Kiksadi clan

fought their last battle against Russian colonizers, who were ruthlessly extending their lucrative fur trade down the coast. The site of the Tlingit fort, its environs, and a Russian memorial are now part of the park. The main walkway behind the beach is an avenue of tall stately trees and Haida totem poles brought to Sitka in 1905. Some resting places and picnic sites are found on grass swards in front of the trees and above the beach. A wheelchair-accessible toilet is on the east bank of Indian River. Aerobic exercise stations are set up for the energetic along the walks on the east bank. A sweep of mountains encircles the bay on three sides, with the restless Pacific on the southwestern skyline. The NPS headquarters is located at the entrance of the park.

From town, walk about a mile east along Lincoln Street to its end, past the small boat harbor and Sheldon Jackson College. The park headquarters is adjacent to the beach. It holds a Native workshop and a museum. Visitors are encouraged to go inside, register, learn about the park, see the artifacts, and watch the artisans at work. Walk out of the beach door and turn left along the main pathway lined with totem

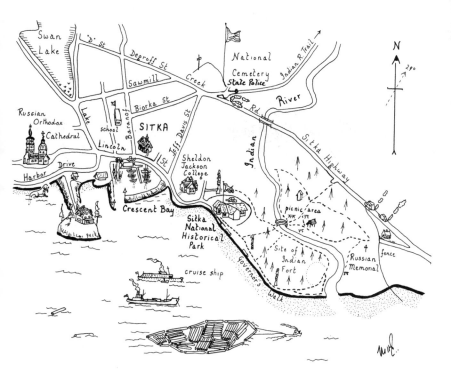

*Totem Walk*

poles. After 5 to 10 minutes the path divides. Turn left for the Tlingit fort site, or right for the mouth of the Indian River and the battle-ground between the Kiksadis and Russians. From the fort site, it is possible to return along Indian River through the woods (see map). A fork from this path crosses Indian River by a footbridge to a picnic area and the exercise stations. A path connects with the Sitka Highway and another path goes southeast to a memorial for Russian midshipmen killed in 1804.

# St5
# INDIAN RIVER

**TIME:** 3 hours
**DISTANCE:** 5 miles
**ELEVATION GAIN:** 1,200 ± feet
**RATING:** moderate
**ACCESS:** 2.5 miles east of Sitka
**TYPE:** fishing, river, forests
**TRAIL CONDITION:** good for first 3.5 miles
**MAP:** Sitka A-4
Avalanche towards end; waterproof boots advisable

This well-defined trail follows Indian River toward its source in the cirque of razor-sharp peaks between the Sisters and Arrowhead Peak. The first mile of this walk is a pleasant stroll along partial board-walk through old-growth forest, perfect for those who wish to go just a short distance. The route passes through selectively logged stands of Sitka spruce. Notches for the logging platforms used years ago may still be visible in the larger stumps. Also watch out for a photogenic patch of skunk cabbage perfectly reflected in a brackish pool; it's at its best in spring. Two salmon species are present in the river, and anglers catch rainbow trout and steelhead. Check with the Alaska Fish and Game Department for periodic species closures. The trail ends in a series of waterfalls. Wear bells or make noise along the route; there is a remote possibility that brown bears are in the vicinity. The trail is maintained by the USFS.

From Crescent Harbor, walk north along Jeff Davis Street to the National Cemetery. Turn right onto Sawmill Creek Road and immediately past the State Trooper's Academy (Department of Public Safety)

*Falls on east fork of Indian River*

turn left. Bear right immediately, go past a gate, and follow a dirt road to its end, 0.7 mile or about a 15-minute walk. The trail starts to the left of a pump house and spillway. It follows the river closely upstream, past deep, clear pools and a series of rapids. After about 0.75 mile, abandon the trail briefly for a detour onto a large muskeg that offers views of Gavan Hill and the Sisters. At 2 miles, cross the north fork of the Indian River. A short distance farther north, cross the east fork.

*Skunk cabbage, Indian River*

The route follows the southeast side of the fork into a deep V-shaped valley, and then crosses back to the opposite bank by a log bridge (no handrail). From this point, the trail deteriorates, but it can be followed through brush and across a slide, which may present an avalanche danger in early spring. The path ends under a waterfall. For greater interest, it is possible to recross the stream and climb up to two higher waterfalls.

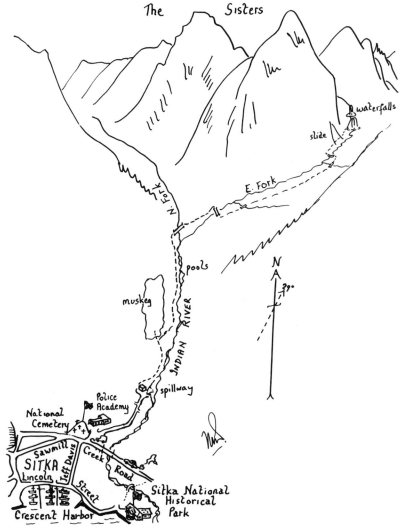

# St6
# BEAVER LAKE

**TIME:** 1.5 hours from pulp mill
**DISTANCE:** 2.5 miles
**ELEVATION GAIN:** 437 feet from tidewater
**RATING:** easy to moderate
**ACCESS:** 6.8 miles east of Sitka
**TYPE:** road, fishing, lake
**TRAIL CONDITION:** good
Avalanche/slide danger on road

Beaver Lake is a small body of water nestled under the sheer flanks of Bear Mountain. It is a good grayling fishing hole, and it has a short 0.7 mile access trail that is partial boardwalk maintained by the

*Beaver Lake*

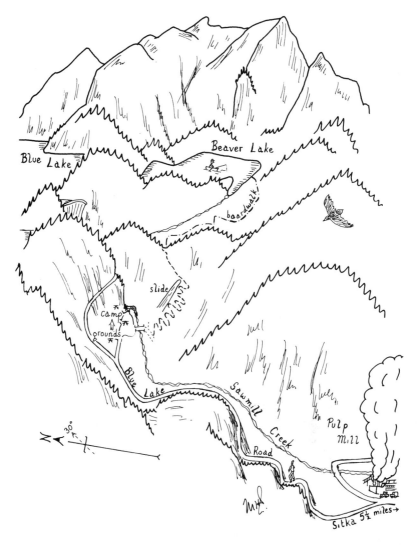

USFS. The approach is by a dirt road that connects Sawmill Creek Road at tidewater, 5 miles east of Sitka, with Blue Lake. Opposite the pulp mill, turn left, and climb steadily, contouring the gorge above Sawmill Creek. At 1.5 miles, a right turn descends to a USFS campground and picnic area below the Blue Lake Dam and spillway. Parking as well as camping is available here, although some people find the short walk up the road more rewarding. The vertical scenery can be enjoyed at leisure. The road is prone to landslides after heavy rains and to avalanche activity in winter.

At the far side of an open area, cross a bridge over Sawmill Creek. The path zigzags steeply and traverses the top end of a slide. Do not attempt to cross the slide partway up. The steep climb is about 200 feet. From the top, a boardwalk runs through mixed forest of hemlock, spruce, and cedar and across muskeg to the lake. The area around the lake is very wet. The outflow into Sawmill Creek provides good fishing.

## St7
# AIRPORT CAUSEWAY

**TIME:** 1.5–2 hours
**DISTANCE:** 1.5 miles
**ELEVATION GAIN:** none
**RATING:** easy
**ACCESS:** small boat
**TYPE:** beach, flowers, World War II relics
**TRAIL CONDITION:** poor
A flashlight is essential; dangerous holes
Stay away from airport

Gun emplacements and military installations were built on the southwest end of a string of islands, west of Sitka airport, to defend the Sitka naval air station in 1941. These were connected by a military road built on a causeway. Since World War II the buildings and access road have fallen into disrepair, and any road left undamaged by wave action is now concealed by heavy brush. Buttercups line the pathway, and the road itself is no more than a footpath under a high arch of alders. Three open, rocky places are a riot of colored carpets—yellow paintbrush (CASTILLEJA UNALASCHCENSIS), fireweed (EPILOBIUM AUGUSTIFOLIUM), bluebells of Scotland (CAMPANULA ROTUNDIFOLIA), and other flora. Just short of Makhnati Island, in the final open area, the road has been obliterated by tidal action and large rocks have been uncovered, making walking awkward. The causeway can be walked in any direction and for any length. The beach is close to hand, and vistas open up to either north or south as the brush permits.

On Makhnati Island, buildings that are thought to have been living quarters, underground powder storage, and a hospital are buried under banks of alder. The buildings are dark, dank, and eerie. One has large, deep holes in the floor that cannot be seen without a light. They pose an extreme hazard. Also watch out for holes elsewhere in the vicinity. Do not take children into this area.

The causeway runs south then west from the airport runway and can be reached by kayak or any small boat. Do not attempt to cross the airport runway. The entire airport perimeter is off-limits to the general public. Be aware of weather changes. A good anchoring beach is found on the west shore of Makhnati Island but is exposed to westerly swells and bad weather. Better protection is found in Whiting Bay. A campsite is found on the west side of Kirushkin Island, but the whole area lacks fresh water.

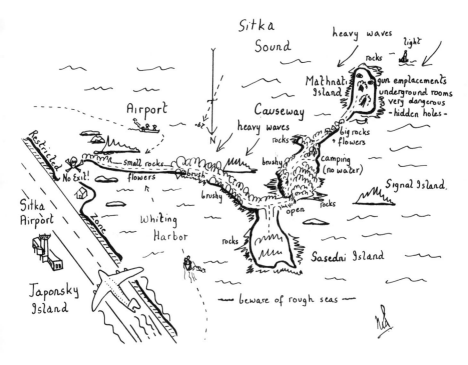

# PETERSBURG

PETERSBURG is a bustling Scandinavian fishing town on Mitkof Island about halfway between Juneau and Ketchikan. It is separated from Kupreanof Island and the city of Kupreanof by a tidal strait called Wrangell Narrows, which is a major shipping lane. The Alaska State ferry makes regular stops, both north- and southbound, and a run through the Narrows is an experience no one should miss. Outstanding peaks, such as the Devils Thumb and Mount Burkett, lie a scant 30 to 40 miles to the northeast and make a splendid backdrop to the wood-frame buildings and fishing harbor. The Le Conte Glacier, an active tidal glacier in the Coast Range 30 miles southeast of Petersburg, is close enough to occasionally bring icebergs to town, when current and winds are right.

Fishing is one of Petersburg's main activities. In summer salmon is caught by seine boat, troller, and sport fishermen, and halibut by longline. There is also seining for herring in the spring, and crabbing and shrimping at various times of year. A tent city was built for cannery workers in 1981, but can be used by any visitor with a tent for a small charge. It includes a covered cooking area, water on tap, and bathroom facilities. It is a good place to meet young people from all over the world. The camp is located southeast of the airport runway, about 0.1 mile west of Sandy Beach. Sandy Beach Recreation Site, southeast of Petersburg, is for day use only, but has covered picnic barbecue areas and picnic tables. About 100 yards south of the picnic grounds, a public boardwalk makes an interesting short walk, jog, or ski run through intervals of trees and muskeg towards Frederick Point.

Mitkof Highway offers a 34-mile drive to Sumner Strait and a view up the Stikine River. About 14 miles south of Petersburg, a short trail gives an unusual view of the Wrangell Narrows, on its way to a popular king salmon fishing hole, Blind River Rapids. Also, from mid-October through March, many trumpeter swans winter in Blind Slough. To facilitate birdwatching without disturbing the wildlife the Forest Service built an observatory overlooking the slough, 16 miles south of town. Even after the swans fly north, there is still abundant wildlife to watch—bald eagles, nesting and migrating ducks, and possibly a black bear fishing in the tidal waters. About half a mile farther south, adjacent to the state's Crystal Lake Hatchery, is Blind Slough picnic area. It has covered picnic tables and swimming beach administered by the

USFS, Petersburg Ranger District. Another 4.5 miles leads to free camping at Ohmer Creek Campground (also USFS).

The city of Kupreanof faces Petersburg across the Wrangell Narrows. An amorphous collection of private homes lines the shoreline. Kupreanof has an excellent local trail system. The city float north of the Alaska State ferry terminal is reached by small boat. City Cab (772-3003) and Scandia Hotel will take people over if prior arrangements are made. The Petersburg Youth Program (772-4422) leads family hikes in the area and welcomes visitors under age 18.

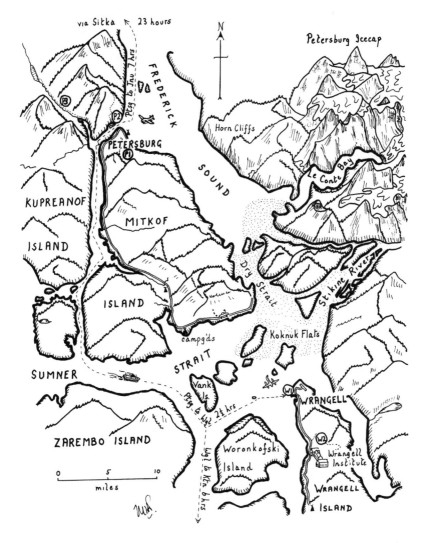

*Frederick Sound and mainland mountains*

## P1
# RAVEN'S ROOST

**TIME:** 2.5 hours
**DISTANCE:** 3.6 miles
**ELEVATION GAIN:** 1,900 feet
**RATING:** moderate
**ACCESS:** foot from town
**TYPE:** muskeg, forest, semi-alpine, ski trail
**TRAIL CONDITION:** good to fair
**MAP:** Petersburg D-3
USFS cabin

Depending on the season, this route offers hiking or intermediate skiing to Raven's Roost, a ski cabin on the 1,745-foot semi-alpine ridgetop south of Petersburg. On clear days the cabin provides distant views of the southern Narrows and Prince of Wales Island. Much of the trail is boardwalk, and it starts in open muskeg meadows with exten-

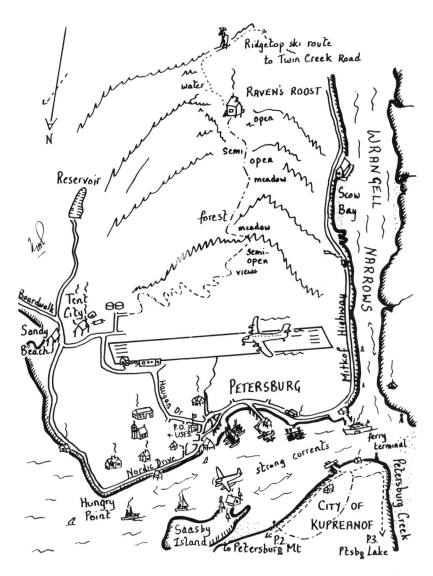

sive views of the Coast Range. There is a steep climb close to the beginning, and a rough section when climbing onto the ridge. At about 1,600 feet, the trail breaks out of trees and opens into expansive views of Frederick Sound, Sukoi Islets, and the ice cap to the northeast.

Overnight visits are recommended in summer and winter. Those planning to stay in the Raven's Roost cabin must register with the USFS. The Petersburg Ranger District office is in town above the post office on Nordic Street. Visitors during mid- to late summer should carry water; after the snows have melted, the nearest spring is about a mile south of the cabin.

Haugen Drive meets Nordic Drive, the main street in Petersburg, between the post office and Hammer Slough. Walk or drive up Haugen Drive to the airport. Continue past the terminal buildings and the east end of the runway to a T junction. Turn right, then take the next left towards a couple of storage tanks. Turn right to limited parking and the start of the boardwalk to Raven's Roost. Views across the muskeg are reached within minutes after ascending through trees. The route climbs more steeply when it re-enters the forest; then it opens to views higher up. Allow a little over an hour to reach the high view-point of Petersburg Mountain and Frederick Sound. From here the route stays close to the ridgetop in trees and goes over two minor summits. Within a mile of the cabin, it finally breaks out into semi-open ridge with views to the southwest. Tree markers are very helpful during snow months, but carefully note each opening, where the route emerges from the forest, for the return. The trail takes unex-pected sharp turns back into the trees from the open areas. Stay alert and keep looking back to the trail opening.

Skiers can continue on a marked route along the ridge over a 2,460-foot summit and descend to the Twin Creek logging road, 3.4 miles from Mitkof Highway. According to rave reviews in the cabin log, this extended ski run offers expanded vistas of the Narrows and Sumner Strait. A more detailed description can be obtained from the Petersburg Ranger District, and an extra topographic map (Petersburg C-3) is needed.

# P2
# PETERSBURG MOUNTAIN

**TIME:** 2.45 hours up, allow full day from town
**DISTANCE:** 2.5 miles
**ELEVATION GAIN:** 2,750 ± feet
**RATING:** strenuous
**ACCESS:** small boat
**TYPE:** mountain, forest
**TRAIL CONDITION:** fair
**MAP:** Petersburg D-3
Tide, strong currents
Tidal tables needed

Petersburg Mountain is the shapely peak north of town across the Wrangell Narrows. In good weather the 360-degree view from the top is panoramic and includes the town of Frederick Sound, the mainland, Kupreanof Island, and the Narrows. The trail is steep and rough, but in contrast, an old moss-covered road that parallels the beach from the city float to the trailhead makes a restful walk between small arching trees.

Those paddling across the Narrows in a canoe or kayak should take the tides into account. Currents are strong at mid-tides. Watch out for larger, powered vessels that have the right-of-way. Take tide tables along and U.S. Coast Guard-approved lighting for the boats. Plan for a complete day for the outing from town. Overnight accommodations are not available on Kupreanof.

Once on the other side, look for the USFS shore marker, indicating public beach access onto the old road west of the southern tip of Saasby Island. The best time to make the crossing is between tides to avoid carrying boats long distances. This is the time that currents are strongest, however, so boaters unsure of their paddling prowess should stay clear of high tidal fluctuations or use the city float during high or low slack. Be sure to carry the boat above the high tide mark before leaving for the day!

Those going to the city float can go almost any time if they are comfortable paddling across strong currents. From here turn right to walk the old road eastward behind the beach. Those feeling energetic can turn left, then right at the next intersection (to Petersburg Creek), then right onto a path signed Petersburg Mountain (see map). This route is a lovely high-level boardwalk through interspersed pines,

*Summit ridge of Petersburg Mountain in fog*

hemlock, and open muskeg. It adds a little over 0.5 mile to the overall mileage but keeps the hiker away from private homes. It joins the road 1 mile east of the float, opposite the path access to the beach. Please respect the property rights of others if walking the beach road.

From the beach access, the road continues for about 0.3 mile, then the trail swings off to the left and starts to climb. The climb is steep and rough, and the trail is muddy in places. Small openings in the trees allow views of Thomas Bay and the Coast Range. When the ridge is reached, turn left (southwest) and climb through small openings and by a dark pool where the ground is very wet. Here the route climbs steeply and becomes a scramble over steep rock. A cable is helpful on the steepest section. From here views are toward Del Monte Peak; the stunning views of town and Wrangell Narrows do not appear until the highest point is reached.

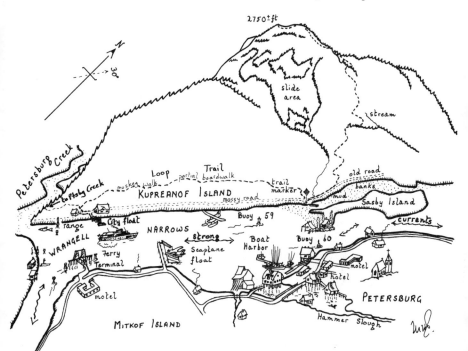

---

## P3
# PETERSBURG CREEK

**TIME:** 6 hours or overnight from city float;
      3 hours from third cabin, plus a 30-minute boat ride
**DISTANCE TO LAKE:** 10 miles; 5.5 miles from third cabin
**ELEVATION GAIN:** insignificant
**RATING:** moderate
**ACCESS:** small boat
**TYPE:** tidal estuary, fishing, forest, lake
**TRAIL CONDITION:** good
**MAPS:** Petersburg D-3 and D-4
Hiking distance dependent on tides
USFS cabin

Petersburg Creek, a few minutes west of Petersburg, is an estuarine river and a favorite fishing hole. Take a fishing pole for most Pacific salmon species, trout, and steelhead casting. Do not compete

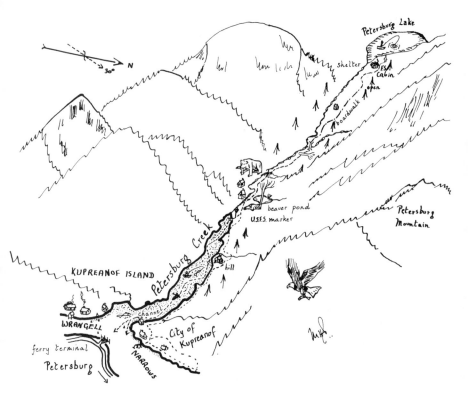

with any black bears that may also be fishing the area. Withdraw immediately and give them room. Waterfowl—many types of ducks and geese—use the bay for breeding and feeding. On a high high tide, hikers can get within fishing distance of the non-tidal creek and within walking distance of Petersburg Lake. Allow 30 minutes by fast boat from town to Third Cabin or at least 60 minutes paddling time, depending on tides. Put tide tables into the pack.

Hikers can choose any of the following options. Arrange for someone with a small boat to take the party the 4.5 miles to the west end of the tidal zone (third cabin) on a high high tide. Look for a USFS trail marker on the right shore showing the location of the trail. The distance to Petersburg Lake from here is 5.5 miles: on the return, do not forget to add an extra mile or so of walking for pick-up due to tidal fluctuations. Plan to return to the city float (4.5 miles from the third cabin) or arrange to be picked up 1 to 2 miles downstream, depending on the length of stay.

Take one's own boat only as far as the first cabin, 3.5 miles upstream, where there is less trouble refloating it on a low tide. Please respect the rights of property owners and use the trail from here.

Use the Kupreanof city float across Wrangell Narrows and north of the ferry terminal. The city of Kupreanof recently built a complex of boardwalk trails that make a good connection between the city float and Petersburg Creek trail system. The walk is much longer; the shore footpath, however, is worth taking. Those not too ambitious can make a delightful, full day seeing the tidal creek as far as they care, then returning to the float. Arrangement may be made with City Cab or Scandia Hotel to take hikers over. Let them know the time to return for a pick up.

Some people fly into Petersburg Lake, stay overnight, and walk out the next day, but arrangements still need to be made for a boat ride into town. Canoeing or kayaking upstream is another method of getting onto the non-tidal creek trail.

Be sure to take warm clothing, raingear, and extra food in case the trip over in the boat is colder than expected, or the wait for the return boat ride is longer than expected. A fishing pole, with a fishing license, is optional. Coast Guard–approved lights are mandatory after dark for all boats. Be prepared for a strong tidal race through the Narrows at certain stages of the tide and give large vessels plenty of room.

From the Kupreanof city float, turn left, then right at the next turn, then left again where the Petersburg Mountain trail goes right, about 0.2 mile from the float. The route, mainly boardwalk, climbs into muskeg with ponds and scattered pines and drops to Petersburg Creek north of Bayou Point, 0.8 mile from the float. From here the trail follows the shoreline closely, occasionally coming out onto grass flatlands until shortly before the first cabin. The path then goes inland, climbs a 150-foot hill, and crosses an unnamed stream, avoiding privately held beach land. It returns to open, grass tidal flats and continues to the final boat landing.

The trail follows freshwater Petersburg Creek upstream as partial boardwalk, but expect windfalls after winter storms. Pass deep, clear fishing pools, meadows, cabins, and vistas of snow-covered mountains as the trail continues upstream. Cross over beaver ponds, a large side stream, and finally muskeg before reaching the Petersburg cabin. Watch for wolf sign up the creek and for bears in the meadows. Beware of wet boardwalk; it can be very slippery. Chicken wire has been placed on the boards to provide better traction. The cabin is on the southeast end of the lake and is in good shape. One must register with the USFS Petersburg Ranger District before spending a night.

# WRANGELL

WRANGELL has an enviable position at the mouth of the Stikine River. It is fronted by rain-washed islands and tidal waters, on which the light is constantly changing. The river has been a dominant factor in the history of the area and in the siting of Wrangell. It was used as a trading corridor by Tlingit Natives for centuries. Then the Russians and the Hudson Bay Company confronted each other over trade routes early in the nineteenth century. In the late 1800s, American gold seekers successfully used the corridor as a gateway to the Cassiar gold fields. Thus, Wrangell has been a pivotal town since pre-Russian days, and it still retains its air of bustle with the timber industry, tourists in summer, tidewater fishing, and waterfowl and moose hunting on the Stikine flats.

Ketchikan is 100 miles south and Petersburg 35 miles north of Wrangell. The Alaska State ferry makes regular stops at its downtown terminal, and jet service and charter planes use the airport on the east side of the peninsula. The Zimovia Highway runs along the shore to Pats Creek, an unimproved campground 11 miles south of town, and then beyond as a dirt road. Turn left at Pats Creek for Pats Lake, a popular recreation site with a short trail connection to the camping area.

*Petroglyph rubbing, Wrangell*

About 6 miles north of town, within the Stikine Estuary, is Garnet Ledge, accessible by boat or floatplane at the higher tides (15± feet). The garnets found here belong to the Boy Scouts, although all Wrangell children may gather the stones and sell them to tourists. About 26 miles northeast of Wrangell is Chief Shakes Hot Springs, which boasts two bath houses administered by the USFS. It is possible to paddle upstream through narrow sloughs, avoiding the main river, to get to the springs. Paddlers planning to visit the estuary or run the Stikine River should note that many of the USFS cabins in this area have oil stoves, precluding the use of wood fires for drying out and cooking. For more details on the Stikine, contact the USFS Wrangell Ranger District, on Bennett Street (the airport road) in Wrangell.

# W1
# WRANGELL CITY WALK

**TIME:** 3–4 hours total, depending on interest
**DISTANCE:** 3.4 miles total
**ELEVATION GAIN:** 450± feet
**RATING:** easy
**ACCESS:** foot from ferry terminal
**TYPE:** native culture, viewpoint

Wrangell is well laid out, and it is worth a walk just to see the gardens and lawns. Set out on the west-facing slope of Dewey Hill, the town overlooks Sumner Strait and gets late afternoon sun. So what better way to spend the time when in Wrangell than to see the town? Visit Chief Shakes Community House on Shakes Island by the boat harbor, then find a viewpoint from Dewey Hill, which rises directly above the city. Look for petroglyphs (hundreds or thousands of years old; the pundits are not sure) on the beach north of town. Plan to see the petroglyphs from mid- to low tide, so change the order of visitation if tides dictate. Take a camera along.

If time is limited, choose just one destination: Shakes Island, a 15- to 20-minute walk; Mount Dewey summit, about 30 to 40 minutes; and the petroglyphs, a 30-minute walk from the ferry terminal.

From the ferry terminal, turn right along Stikine Avenue, left at the Stikine Inn, then right onto Front Street, through the shopping dis-

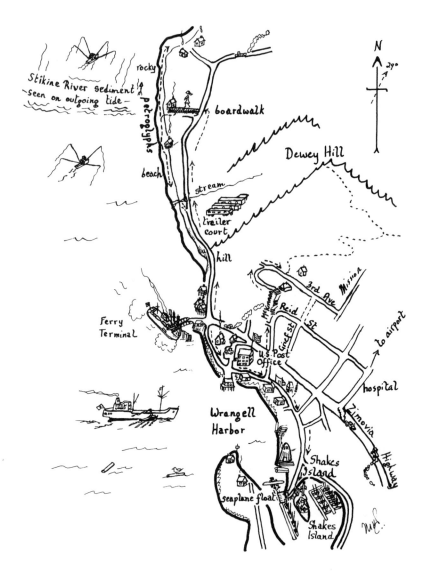

trict. Take Shake Street toward the seaplane float. Shakes Island, with totem poles and a cedar house, is on the left above the boat harbor. Walk across the wooden bridge. The Community House, the central theme of the island, was built in 1930, and it is an example of a high-caste Tlingit Native building. For those wishing to go inside, inquire at the museum or look for the hours posted on the building.

From Shakes Island, turn back along Front Street and take any road up to the next level to Church Street. Turn left and find McKinnon Street, behind the post office on the north end of town. Turn right uphill; continue up on the McKinnon Street staircase. Turn left and follow the road around under the forested slope of the hill (see map). A rough trail on the left goes up through trees to the top of Dewey Hill, about a 20-minute walk. Beware of false trails in the trees going to nearby housing estates. Note the route well for the quick return to Third Street and McKinnon.

Descend to Church Street and turn right behind the post office to return to the ferry terminal (now Second Street). To continue the walk to the petroglyphs, turn right along the shore and walk north for 0.6 mile, over a small hill by a trailer court, and cross a stream. Shortly after, look for a signed boardwalk and short road to the beach. This is public beach access. Take care if the boards are wet. Look carefully for markings in the large beach rocks, especially those to the north. Some of the better ones have been taken to the Wrangell Museum for safekeeping, but good examples of the petroglyphs remain here. Take photographs, or better yet, put the camera away and place a sheet of paper over the carving. Rub with charcoal or crayon to get an impression. Do not chalk the petroglyphs themselves to highlight the design; this defaces the carving and is illegal. It also defeats the purpose by making any photograph less authentic.

# W2
# RAINBOW FALLS

**TIME:** 45 minutes
**DISTANCE:** 0.8 mile
**ELEVATION GAIN:** 450 feet
**RATING:** easy to moderate
**ACCESS:** 4.6 miles Zimovia Highway
**TYPE:** falls, forest
**TRAIL CONDITION:** good

The trail to Rainbow Falls was built in the 1930s by the Civilian Conservation Corps (CCC). It has become a favorite walk for the local

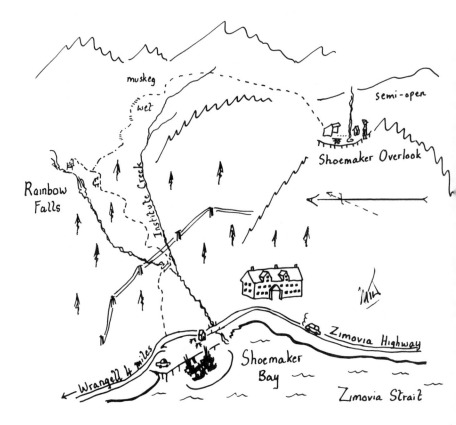

folks. Recently, the trail was extended by the USFS, up Institute Creek to a semi-open ridgetop suitable for cross-country skiing and a viewpoint of Zimovia Strait and Shoemaker Bay. The first 200 hundred yards of trail are characterized by large hemlock trees, decaying ferns, a mossy floor, and moss-covered stumps. The trail starts across from Shoemaker Bay and a small boat harbor 4.6 miles south of Wrangell.

The route goes through tall trees and crosses a tributary of Institute Creek within a powerline slash. Then it stays on a ridge above both streams and climbs to a viewpoint of the falls. Tree roots help to form steps up the small ridge. Go a little farther (0.2 mile) to get to the top of the falls and a viewpoint of Woronkofski Island.

*Along the trail to Rainbow Falls*

# SHOEMAKER HILL

**TIME:** 2.5 hours
**DISTANCE:** 3.5 miles
**ELEVATION GAIN:** 1,700 feet
**TYPE:** view lookout, subalpine
**TRAIL CONDITION:** good to fair
**MAPS:** Petersburg B-1 and B-2

Those going on should wear strong, waterproof boots.

Between the viewpoint and falls, a trail goes to the right and follows Institute Creek upstream. The initial 0.5 mile was surfaced with native cedar materials in 1985 and 1989. It climbs steadily through woods, past small waterfalls, eventually emerging into a series of muskegs. The tread is very wet and boggy wherever there is no boardwalk. It crosses over Institute Creek and climbs south then west through semi-open country to the ridge. At the top is a three-sided Adirondack shelter with a sleeping bench, fire pit, picnic table, outhouse, and a magnificent view.

# KETCHIKAN

KETCHIKAN is the hub of southern Southeast Alaska. From here connections are made to the villages and logging camps of Prince of Wales Island and Annette Island. Floatplanes go to Meyer's Chuck, the Unuk River, Hyder, and Misty Fjords on the mainland, and to wilderness lakes, cabins, and hot springs on the northern, or back, end of Revillagigedo Island ("Revilla" for short). Ketchikan is an exciting, lively town, with a huge independent fishing fleet, a pulp mill, a rich Native cultural heritage, and a frontage of amphibious airlines. Ketchikan is long and narrow and faces the partially protected waters of the Tongass Narrows. Its whole width is taken up by houses, staircases, and wood-slatted streets that are perched precariously on steep, wooded hillsides and lend a unique charm to the town.

The main airport is across the Tongass Narrows, on Gravina Island, with a half-hourly ferry service connection. Jet flights connect with Juneau, Sitka, Anchorage, Seattle, and points south. Hikers may walk around the southeast airport perimeter to gain access to Gravina Island, but they must check in and out at the ferry toll booth. Roads on Revilla Island extend 20 miles north and 14 miles south. Visitors can camp north of town at Ward Lake; Last Chance about 2 miles north of Ward Lake; or Settlers Cove, at the end of the road. The Alaska Marine Highway terminal is 1.5 miles north of the town center and is linked by regular bus service. Cruise ships also dock in town.

Ketchikan may seem small to many visitors, but it has a "rush hour" that lasts all day. The traffic hangups are sometimes beyond belief, so be careful as you walk downtown, and obey traffic signals. Motorists are generally courteous to pedestrians and recognize crossings long after the paint has faded. A walk around town is highly recommended, along with visits to the museum, Creek Street, hatchery, and in season, the fish ladder. Those with transportation should not miss the village of Saxman or the Totem Bight.

Low-level trails give the visitor a feel for this area's magnificent climax forests, where Sitka spruce, western hemlock, and cedar arch high overhead, and an eye-level understory of devil's club predominates. From the center of town, one can walk up to a viewpoint of Ketchikan and the Tongass Narrows and climb into alpine wilderness, all in one day.

But . . . it rains! The Ketchikan area gets up to 160 inches of rain in a year, and although there are many sunny days, the low-pressure weather systems that chase each other through here can spoil the ridge-top hiking fun. Drinking water is readily available in many alpine areas, unless there has been a long dry spell in September.

Maps required are Ketchikan quadrangles B-5, B-6, and C-5, 1 inch to the mile. Please note that two of these routes (K6 and K7) are for experienced hikers only, preferably those who are already familiar with the local area. The USFS has expressed interest in these routes, and it is hoped they will be formally adopted.

# K1
# DEER MOUNTAIN

**TIME:** 3 hours
**DISTANCE:** 3.3 miles
**ELEVATION GAIN:** 3,001 feet
**RATING:** moderate to strenuous
**ACCESS:** by foot from town
**TYPE:** forest, alpine
**MAP:** Ketchikan B-5
USFS cabins

The pointed peak of Deer Mountain dominates the southeast end of town. The trail is easy to find and follow and, although wet in places, it offers an uninterrupted view of town, the Tongass Narrows, and the islands to the north and west of 2,400 feet elevation. Two USFS cabins at alpine have been damaged by vandals, which is unfortunate, because the Blue Lake cabin is especially valuable as a weather shelter. Inquire of the USFS about the status of both cabins before using them. In late summer, when the pool is ice free, take a fishing pole along to Blue Lake for grayling.

From the center of town, find Ketchikan Creek on Stedman Street. Walk past Thomas Basin and take the first road to the left, Deermont Street. Go up a short hill, keep right, and walk to a T junction at its end. Turn right onto a dirt road posted to the sanitary landfill, and climb a steep hill with sharp curves to a junction at the top. To the right is the sanitary landfill and to the left is Ketchikan Lakes. Turn left, and within a few yards look for the Deer Mountain trailhead on the right.

The path crosses muskeg to the base of the peak. Then it climbs in forest by a series of zigzags to a view of Annette Island and Nichols Passage, at about 1,500 feet elevation. In late summer, the last stream is crossed a short way farther on, and the trees become shorter and sparser as the trail reaches the 2,000-foot level. Look below for a view of the Tlingit village of Saxman. The steepness diminishes, and at about 600 feet below the summit, there is a broad "platform" viewpoint giving expansive views of Ketchikan, the Tongass Narrows, and Gravina and Prince of Wales islands.

The trail climbs above a pool and divides. When avalanche danger is high on the exposed north slope of Deer Mountain, take the right fork into dwarf mountain hemlock trees for the Deer Mountain sum-

*Ketchikan and Tongass Narrows from Deer Mountain*

mit. The left fork traverses an exposed north-facing slope that is prone to avalanche in winter and early spring, but it is a lovely walk across carpets of alpine flowers in late summer. It leads directly onto the ridge linking Deer Mountain with the Fin (an adjacent peak less than 0.5 mile north-northeast of Deer Mountain). This is the best way to Blue Lake and the most accessible route to the Deer Mountain cabin (300 feet below and east of the peak), although it is possible to scramble from the summit to the cabin.

## BLUE LAKE

**TIME:** 4.5 hours from Ketchikan
**DISTANCE:** 5.1 miles
**ELEVATION GAIN:** 3,600 feet
    To continue to Blue Lake, descend 100 to 150 feet below and to

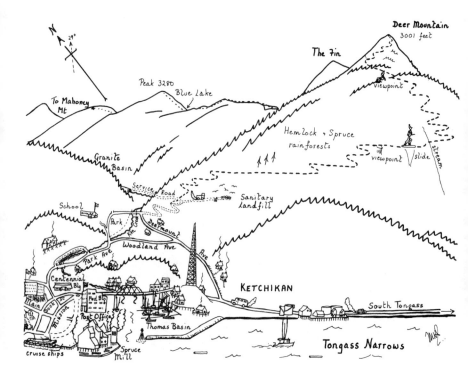

the east of the Fin, and travel north-northeast. (Do not forget the huge compass declination of 29 degrees east.) Regain the ridge about 0.75 mile farther. Energetic hikers can scramble over the Fin, but this route is not recommended when snows linger. The trail has acquired a tread over the years, and the Forest Service has put up metal posts along the ridge, making it easier to follow. The route climbs gently over a 3,001 foot summit with uninterrupted views of islands, mountains, distant ice caps in all directions, and a shining copper sea under the sun to the south and west. The lake and cabin are concealed in a shallow basin 400 feet beneath the end of the ridge.

Visitors be warned! The ridge is exposed to bad weather, and one can get lost, cold, and wet without the right equipment. In addition to the Ten Essentials, take an ice ax for the snow slope below the Deer Mountain summit. Beware of ridge cornices; stay away from the edge. Do not attempt to escape the ridge by dropping into Granite Basin.

Experienced hikers can continue north along the ridge to Upper Mahoney Basin and descend to Silvis Lakes and Beaver Falls by the Mahoney Mountain Trail (K2).

# K2
# MAHONEY MOUNTAIN

**TIME:** 3.5 hours from Beaver Falls
**DISTANCE:** 4.5 miles
**ELEVATION GAIN:** 3,400 feet
**RATING:** strenuous
**ACCESS:** Beaver Falls, 14 miles north of Ketchikan
**TYPE:** alpine
**TRAIL CONDITION:** poor
**MAP:** Ketchikan B-5

Mahoney and John mountains are situated on the north end of the ridge above Ketchikan in some outstanding country. The two peaks are separated by an ice-sculptured alpine basin and a sprinkling of tarns that are snow-covered much of the year; the northerly ones are known locally as Iceberg Lakes. But by August the area is thickly carpeted with alpine flowers. Attractive camping (but exposed to storm winds) is found almost anywhere in the basin above Upper Mahoney Lake, although snow persists longer in the higher elevations of the south end. The slopes into the basin are steep, so reaching the north end presents a challenge when the upper tarn is free of ice. A topographic map and compass are essential for steering through this high country.

Beaver Falls is reached by driving to the end of South Tongass Highway, and the trailhead approached by the Ketchikan Public Utilities (KPU) road to Lower Silvis Lake. Before the 1969 landslide, which obliterated the old hillside, a road connected Lower Silvis Lake with Upper Silvis Lake, and the Mahoney Mountain trail started from the dam at Upper Silvis. Now, foot traffic is tolerated on the road to the lower lake, and hikers may cross in front of a small powerhouse at the west end to a rough route that climbs steeply to bypass Upper Silvis Lake. Motor traffic is not allowed on the road. Only strong, well-prepared walkers should consider crossing the high-level basin west of Mahoney Mountain to reach John Mountain. Sudden weather changes could dictate an unplanned bivouac in the basin, and fog or snow could make the route off the mountain tricky to find. A high-level traverse to Ketchikan, via Blue Lake (see K1), is possible. Take camping

*Upper Iceberg Lakes and John Mountain from Mahoney Mountain*

gear, including a cooking stove, and enough food for two to three days. These routes are maintained by the USFS, Ketchikan Ranger District.

Drive south along South Tongass Highway 14 miles to its end at Beaver Falls. Parking is limited. Walk through some gates, past a power station, and sign the register placed in the forecourt. Follow the KPU

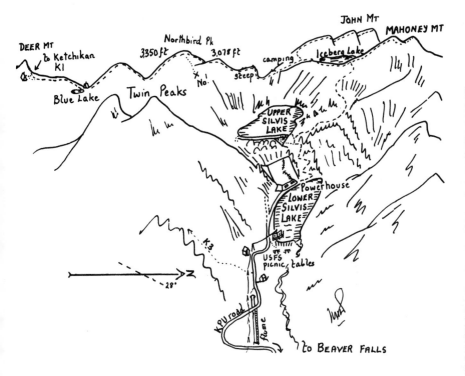

dirt road that starts to the left beyond the buildings. It climbs steeply, then more gradually, for about 2 miles to Lower Silvis Lake. Find the trail beyond the upper powerhouse at the end of the road. It zigzags steeply toward Upper Silvis Lake and meets the original route (mentioned above) about 150 feet above the dam. Going up, it is easy to miss the short, steep connecting path onto the old trail. People mistakenly traverse the hill, then drop into a gully beneath the dam. If this happens, climb onto the dam, enjoy the view, have a late breakfast, then turn right towards the hill. The original path starts at the end of the dam, climbs towards the right, and meets the new route.

The trail is in poor shape. It is wet in places; it is also poorly marked and makes sharp turns that are not always easy to figure out. The trail crosses small ravines in three places; care should be taken here to stay on the correct trail. The route climbs in forest up a broad ridge to a small bowl at the upper treeline. As trees get smaller, look back to be sure the route can be found on the return. The bowl, at about 2,300 feet elevation, offers adequate camping with running water. The route climbs up the left (south) rim, staying above steep drop-offs into the Upper Silvis Lake Basin, and gradually climbs to the Mahoney Mountain Ridge. Metal posts that mark the route may be visible on open slopes, but they are often knocked down by heavy snowfall and can be lost in foul weather.

The trail joins the ridge at about 3,000 feet with views southeast into Upper Silvis Basin, and west-northwest to John Mountain. Go north-northeast, up the gently sloping ridge, to reach Mahoney Mountain, 3,350 feet above sea level.

# JOHN MOUNTAIN

**TIME:** 4.5 hours from Beaver Falls
**DISTANCE:** 5.6 miles
**ELEVATION GAIN:** 4,600 feet round trip
**TRAIL CONDITION:** nebulous

To get onto the south ridge of John Mountain, go southwest and descend 450 feet to the south end of the Upper Mahoney Basin (the high country between Mahoney and John mountains). Cross the basin and climb onto the ridge, which is steep and generally snow-covered into June. By mid-July, it is a riot of alpine flowers and small snowmelt pools. A sharp drop of about 70 feet before the final summit is awkward, with loose slab and mossy rock after the snow has gone.

# BEAVER FALLS TO KETCHIKAN

**TIME:** 2–3 days
**DISTANCE:** 12 miles
**ELEVATION GAIN:** 5,100 feet
**TRAIL CONDITION:** nebulous

Follow the Mahoney Mountain trail (K2) to the ridge. Descend to the south end of Upper Mahoney Basin. Check position with topo map.

Go south from the basin towards a notch in the John Mountain-Blue Lake Ridge. This includes a gentle descent to a tiny tarn with a clear running stream and dwarf mountain hemlock, which give some shelter—a beautiful campsite. Another couple of hundred feet down is the notch (about 2,350 feet elevation). From here, expect a steep climb of about 250 feet, through trees, then exposed slab. Use the ropes, placed on the steep section by the USFS for balance only. The ridge ascends gently over a couple of tops, then a short, steep snow slope brings one to the 3,350 foot summit of Northbird Peak. (Northbound travelers must be sure to keep northwest, when coming off the peak. Gentle snow slopes look inviting towards the northeast, but these drop abruptly into the deep basin above Upper Silvis Lake.) The ridge then is pleasant walking over a 3,280-foot summit to Blue Lake. Continue south-southwest along the ridge to Deer Mountain and descend to Ketchikan by the Deer Mountain trail (K1).

Those going north may stay a night at Blue Lake and reach Beaver Falls the next day. Make arrangements for car pick up to return to town.

# K3
# TWIN PEAKS

**TIME:** 3 hours from Beaver Falls
**DISTANCE:** 2.5 miles
**ELEVATION GAIN:** 3,370 feet
**RATING:** strenuous
**ACCESS:** Beaver Falls, 14 miles south of Ketchikan
**TYPE:** forest, muskeg, alpine
**TRAIL CONDITION:** tagged route only
**MAP:** Ketchikan B-5
Experienced hikers only

Two graceful peaks are visible from the northbound ferry as it steams across Carroll Inlet toward Mountain Point and Ketchikan. Called Twin Peaks, they present sweeping views of mountains, inlets, islands, and distant seascapes. In winter and spring, an ice ax is needed for the summit ridges. From the road there is no trail; it is a route tagged by local residents and should only be attempted by experienced hikers.

From the ferry terminal, turn right through town and follow South Tongass Highway to its end at Beaver Falls, about 14 miles. Parking is limited. Walk through some gates, past a power station, and up the KPU service road, which climbs steeply round a couple of S bends. After about 45 minutes of walking (about 1.5 miles), and about 3 minutes after passing some falls on the right, look for a bog meadow on the left. A few yards beyond this (shortly before a small stream crossing), turn left, walk under the powerlines, and cross a strip of muskeg into

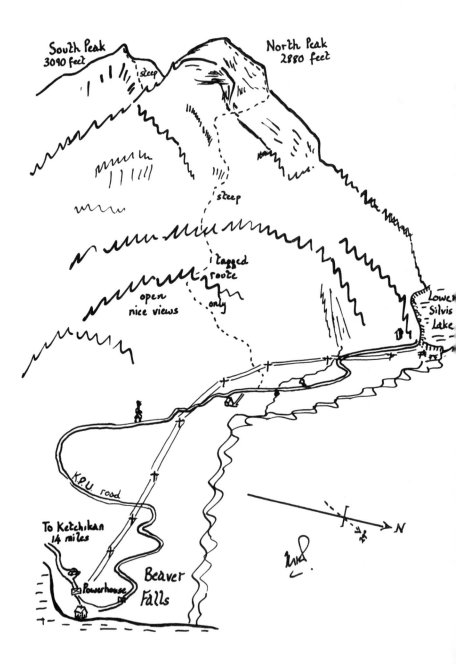

South Peak
3090 feet

steep

North Peak
2880 feet

steep

tagged
route
only

open
nice views

Lower
Silvis
Lake

K.P.U. road

To Ketchikan
14 miles

Powerhouse

Beaver
Falls

N

the trees. The route climbs through trees and small openings and ends on the edge of a series of muskegs. Head for the immediate ridge to pleasant, low-level views of surrounding mountains and inlets. It is easy to get lost here. Note the route for the return.

Go in a southwesterly direction and, if care is taken, follow the flagging up the lower slopes of the north peak. The route goes past some blowdowns and continues almost straight up to the right of a stream trickle before it emerges into a steep meadow. Check the return route here and once again when the high alp is reached under the summit of the north peak. Lower Silvis Lake should be directly below, but is not seen because slope and tall trees get in the way. Traverse westward across the open slope to the skyline ridge. From here there are lovely views of Mahoney Mountain and Upper Silvis Lake. Follow the ridge to the summit of the north peak, 2,880 feet elevation. The south peak, about 0.3 mile away, is separated by a saddle 200 feet lower than the north peak. Beware when snow lingers. The summit route is steep and dangerous.

# K4
# WARD LAKE

**TIME:** 30–50 minutes (circuit)
**DISTANCE:** 1.6 miles (circuit)
**ELEVATION GAIN:** none
**RATING:** easy
**ACCESS:** 8.5 miles northwest of Ketchikan
**TYPE:** nature walk
**TRAIL CONDITION:** excellent

Ward Lake is 1 mile northeast of Ward Cove. It is a favorite USFS camping and picnic site for local residents and visitors from Outside. It is renown for its giant cedars and Sitka spruce, and in unusually cold winters, it becomes the local skating rink. A covered picnic area on the north shore is for large parties. Individual picnic sites are scattered along the east shore. Signal Creek Campground is on the south end; 3-Cs Campground is on Ward Creek; and Last Chance Campground is 1.8 miles farther up the road. All are administered by the USFS Ketchikan Ranger District.

Turn left from the Ketchikan ferry terminal and take the shore road (North Tongass Highway) to Ward Cove, which, with the presence of the pulp mill, is unmistakable. At the head of the cove, turn right up a dirt road to Ward Lake and park where space is provided by the picnic area on the north end. Walk through the picnic grounds and follow the lakeshore. Watch for huge trees, some bent and "woven" into odd shapes. Also note the evidence of past selective cutting along the west shoreline above the footpath. Tree seedlings have taken root in some old stumps, and many other stumps are covered with bracket fungi, some the bright color splash of chicken-in-the-woods.

A williwaw (fierce circular wind) uprooted a number of trees on the west side of the lake outflow, probably during the 1968 Thanksgiving Day storm. Follow the lakeshore through the campgrounds on the south end and take a leisurely tour of the magnificent spruce, hemlock, and yellow and red cedar found by the road. Bald eagles and ravens are a common sight, and ravens, especially, give the forest its particular ambience, with honks, bell tones, and screams.

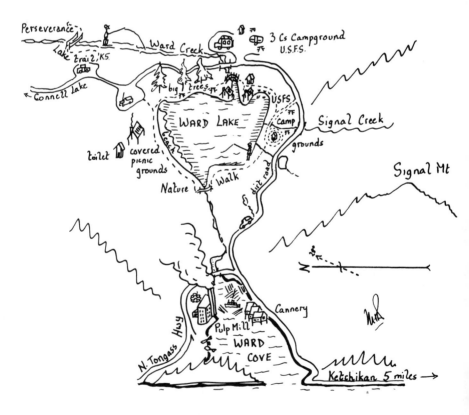

*Ward Lake Trail*

<table>
<tr><td></td><td>K5</td><td></td></tr>
</table>

# PERSEVERANCE LAKE

**TIME:** 1 hour
**DISTANCE:** 1.7 miles
**ELEVATION GAIN:** 750 feet
**RATING:** easy
**ACCESS:** 8.5 miles northwest of town
**TYPE:** forest, muskeg
**TRAIL CONDITION:** varies

Take a fishing pole to catch trout in Perseverance Lake. The boardwalk placed there by the USFS is pleasant in summer for casual visitors with nothing better than tennis shoes. The walk has recently been repaired, eliminating rotten areas.

Go to Ward Lake (see K4). A few yards past the Ward Lake picnic area there is parking on the right. The Perseverance Lake Trail starts here, goes down a hill, and crosses Ward Creek on a suspension bridge. It is hard to lose and climbs steadily through forest and up a stream draw into muskeg. There are views of Ward and Juno mountains to the south, and Diana Mountain to the east. The trail enters trees once more and finally crosses the Perseverance Lake outflow. The lake itself is about 200 yards farther on.

It is possible for experienced hikers to climb onto the west ridge of Diana Mountain, 3,014 feet high, from the north end of the lake. The route is unmarked and steep at first, but by careful navigation, a way may be found through the short bluffs. Once the ridge is gained, remember the route for the return. The trees then quickly disappear, and it is a comparatively simple hike to the summit. Those going all the way need all Ten Essentials and Ketchikan B-5 topographic map.

## K6
# CONNELL LAKE AND BROWN MOUNTAIN

**TIME:** 3 hours
**DISTANCE:** 2.8 miles
**ELEVATION GAIN:** 3,200 feet
**RATING:** strenuous
**ACCESS:** 11 miles north of town
**TYPE:** forest, alpine
**TRAIL CONDITION:** no trail from Talbot Lake
**MAPS:** Ketchikan B-5 and B-6
Backcountry experts only

Brown Mountain, 2,978 feet, is the most northerly of a triad of peaks that encircle a subalpine plateau, known locally as SEAMA Basin. The basin is approximately 2,400 feet above sea level and contains three or four small lakes not marked on the map. It has scant tree cover, but otherwise offers attractive wilderness camping. The difficulty is getting there. The Forest Service is interested in mapping out a

*Stream crossing, Connell Lake Trail*

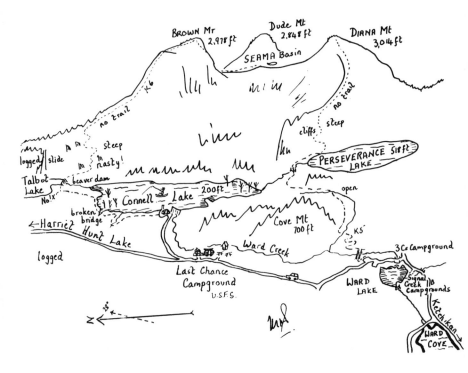

trail system over Brown Mountain and possibly a connecting route to
Ward Mountain, when time and money permit. Till then, hikers must
use their route-finding skills to get to the Brown Mountain ridge, then
traverse the peak to get to the country behind. The trip is well worth
the trouble, but it will take a long day, or overnight, to get to Diana or
Dude mountains, and return to Connell Lake.

Drive the dirt road to Ward Lake (see K4) and turn right at the
first major intersection for Connell Lake (2.3 miles from Ward Lake).
The Connell Lake Trail is visible at the end of the parking area to the
left of the dam. The trail follows the west shore of the lake, and it is
good for about the first 20 minutes. Turn left at a trail intersection.
Soon the trail deteriorates into brush and broken boardwalk and may
even be lost at some broken bridge diversions. At the fourth bridge
crossing, there is a pleasant camping area in big trees. At bridge number 12, there may be some difficulty finding the trail across a gully.
Glimpses of the lake are rare, and, at one point, a clearcut to the Harriet Hunt Road is visible through the trees. (Steer clear of clearcuts.
They are a struggle.)

When the path reaches Talbot Lake, clearcuts to the lake can be seen, and the boardwalk has collapsed causing danger to pedestrians. Leave the boardwalk shortly before the south end of Talbot Lake and cross the river flowing out of the lake by a beaver dam. Climb eastward onto the north ridge of Brown Mountain. The way is steep and presents some route-finding challenges around bluffs and fallen trees; but it is possible. One suggestion is to use surveyor's ribbon to mark the route. Please take it out during the return. Walking is pleasant once the ridge is attained, and at about 1,800 feet, an open muskeg containing a pool straddles the ridge. Climbing steepens in trees, and one can either go to right or left of a gully that splits the ridge. The upper slopes are broad, gentle, and open to extensive views.

Brown Mountain summit has fragile muskeg surrounded by mountain hemlock and juniper thickets, but north of the immediate summit are swales and hillocks, melting snow, scattered hemlocks, and great camping. To reach SEAMA Basin, go over Brown Mountain and descend on the west side of the summit ridge where it stays more open. Groves of small trees get in the way, but with careful searching, ways can be found around them. When the ridge drops off more steeply, a natural route goes to the right (west) and threads its way under bluffs and over an exposed face. Once at SEAMA Basin, the walk onto Diana Mountain (about 1.2 miles from Brown Mountain) has only minor difficulties—large slabs at the bottom of the ridge—in good weather. From the top there are extensive views of Ward Cove, Connell Lake, Cleveland Peninsula, and Prince of Wales Island. On the south side of the peak, Ketchikan Lakes lie immediately below, and Ketchikan can be seen in the distance. Dude Mountain, the third peak to the southeast, is another prominent viewpoint.

Note: Trail conditions can change. Check with the USFS Ketchikan Ranger District before hiking onto Brown Mountain and into SEAMA Basin. Do not attempt to descend to Perseverance Lake from the east ridge of Diana Mountain, unless the route is already familiar to members of the group.

# K7
# WOLF LAKES

**TIME:** 7 hours
**DISTANCE:** 6.8 miles
**ELEVATION GAIN/LOSS:** 1,200 feet
**RATING:** moderately difficult
**ACCESS:** small boat to Moser Bay; road to Harriet Hunt Lake
**TYPE:** tideland, lake, forest, valley and hill muskeg
**TRAIL CONDITION:** poor to Wolf Lakes, non-existent
**MAPS:** Ketchikan B-5 and C-5
Backcountry experts only
USFS three-sided shelter

The trail to Wolf Lakes from Moser Bay, 2.6 miles, visits interesting country between Naha and Harriet Hunt Lake. Upper Wolf Lake offers good cutthroat fishing. Deer and black bear inhabit the area, and large populations of wolf are evident especially during winter. There are route-finding difficulties, however, and local help may be needed for transportation. The USFS trail is nebulous between tidewater and Lower Wolf Lake, and the route between Upper Wolf Lake and Harriet Hunt Lake "uplands" is not easy to find the first time through.

The approach from the north is by small boat to Moser Bay 10.5 miles from Knudsen Cove or 25 road and sea miles (15 air miles) from Ketchikan. Protected waters make access fairly easy, except under bad weather conditions. The USFS trail starts at the mouth of the Lower Wolf Lake River, about a quarter of the way down the east shore of the bay. Trail markers are not easily seen from the water, so a map or chart will be useful for location.

The route is described from north to south; the destination being the road end at Harriet Hunt Lake, 17 road miles north of Ketchikan. This is reached by driving 7 miles past the Ward Lake picnic grounds (see K4). Keep going straight at the Connell Lake turn, then turn left at the next intersection. Leave a car here for the return into town.

The trail to Upper Wolf Lake is wet over much of its length and is marked by tree blazes and flagging. At first, it runs east past a couple of small ponds, then it climbs a small hill and emerges into muskeg, where the route may be difficult to follow. Be careful not to be misled

*Remains of a cedar tree after a williwaw (Photo by Bob Fernbach)*

by surveying activity. The trail goes east-southeast, then east, to Lower Wolf Lake, 1.7 miles from the beach. Follow the lakeshore, then the stream at its south end, for about 0.25 mile. Cross the stream on a log, which is not immediately apparent. The route then runs up the east bank of the stream through bog, muskeg, woods, and meadow. In

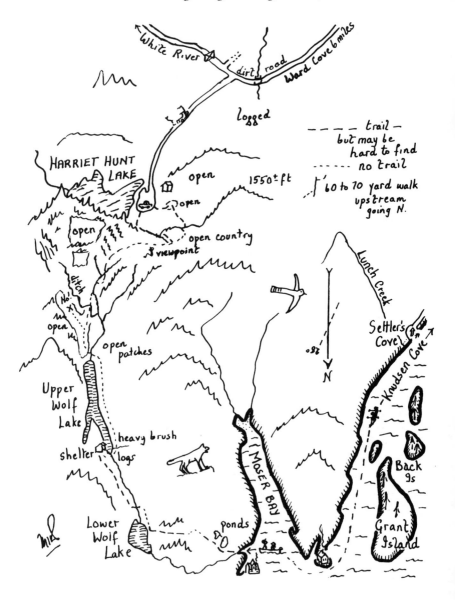

places, the way is not easily seen, but it can be followed by maintaining a consistent southeasterly direction. A three-sided shelter will be found at the north end of the west arm of Upper Wolf Lake. It is in good condition, except for the boggy floor.

From here, find a route across a logjam at the north end of the upper lake. Then go through groves of devil's club and brush into an open area close to the west shore. Continue south through three thickets, more open patches, and across a stream. Then finally cross the main stream, which runs into Upper Wolf Lake at its south end, and enter a large meadow. From here the high land above Harriet Hunt Lake forms the southern skyline, and the route heads towards the lowest area in the center, where open upland muskegs are found (186 degrees true compass bearing). Go south through the large open area, but do not follow it to the end. Within 0.5 mile, flagging and a path of sorts may be seen leading southwest in semi-open country across a ditch to a stream. This is not easily seen unless flagging is obvious. The path disappears in a welter of brush and devil's club, so walk up the stream about 60 yards and look for a marked route that starts on the right (west) bank. It may be hard to find, so keep looking. (If you get lost, don't worry, you are in good company. Have a cookie and a sandwich, then get out the map and compass and follow a southerly course uphill to open muskeg.) The path follows the stream through forest and re-crosses it higher up. The route then goes uphill between two streams, through a semi-open muskeg and forest and emerges in the hill muskeg. From here Wolf Lake and the country just traversed can be seen below.

Go southwest for about 0.25 mile, descending gently over open country toward a 1,600 foot tree-covered hill. Cross a ditch, then look for trail markings to the left. If these are missed, ski marks and all-terrain-vehicle trails will be seen closer to the hill heading downward toward Harriet Hunt Lake. The latter trail is easy to follow once found, but it is wet and awkward underfoot. Logs have been thrown down to create a bed for skiers and winter vehicles.

Those going north from the parking lot at Harriet Hunt Lake have the choice of following the trail or going immediately left and uphill onto the skiers' "roadway." If taking the latter, more direct route, climb along the opening to muskeg and look for the route going to the right. Then continue upward to open country. For the trail, follow the lake shore from the parking lot on wet rough pathway. It crosses a stream and climbs into muskeg. Where the trail leaves the trees and enters the first of a series of muskegs and pools, good views are obtained south over Harriet Hunt Lake and John Mountain. Both routes end in the open muskeg fairly close to each other on top. Head northeast across open country as far as is possible without entering trees. A shallow gully with a wall of trees on the east side leads downward onto the Wolf Lake Trail. Follow this down until wet trail tread is seen.

Note: Flagging is inconsistent and may change from year to year. Hikers who know the route should continue to clear and mark the way.

*Sitka spruce*

---
## K8
# NAHA
---

**TIME:** 3.5 hours from tidal float; overnight from Ketchikan
**DISTANCE:** 6 miles
**ELEVATION GAIN:** 450 ± feet
**RATING:** easy to moderate
**ACCESS:** small boat or floatplane, 18 miles north of Ketchikan
**TYPE:** salt- and freshwater lagoons, river, lakes
**TRAIL CONDITION:** excellent to good
**MAP:** Ketchikan C-5
Take fishing poles
USFS cabin at Jordan Lake and Heckman Lake

Naha is Ketchikan's crown jewel. There is a blending of seawater chucks and freshwater lagoons; salmon, cutthroat, steelhead, and rainbow fishing; and old-growth forest. For good reason, it is a very popular place. The area is reached by small boat from Knudson Cove, 15 miles northwest of town or by direct floatplane flight from Ketchikan to Roosevelt Lagoon, or Jordan or Heckman lakes. Experienced kayakers can paddle up the 9 miles of coast from Settler's Cove at the end of the North Tongass Highway. They go up the lagoon to Naha River Falls, immediately beyond Orton Ranch. Orton Ranch is a Boy Scout camp found about 0.25 mile east of Roosevelt Lagoon. It is private property, so visitors should keep to the trail when walking by.

The mileage quoted in the heading is to the Heckman Lake USFS cabin. The Naha River shelter and campsite is 2.5 miles, and Jordan Lake cabin is 4 miles from tidewater. Plan on an overnight stay when coming from Ketchikan and avoid weekends if possible because it is a popular outing spot with locals. Take camping gear or reserve a cabin well in advance during the summer season.

There is sheltered anchorage within Naha Bay. Small craft can be taken into Roosevelt Lagoon by using a tramway between tides when the tidal falls are active. A 15-foot or greater tide is needed to paddle through during high slack. An alternative is a trail, mainly boardwalk, that hugs the shoreline of the lagoon and goes through stands of Sitka spruce, skunk cabbage, and dogwood. Seals, loons, mergansers, and other wildlife may be seen in the bay and upper lagoon (seals swim in during high water). Covered camping, picnic tables, and toilets are located close to the tramway and at the Naha River campsite at the east

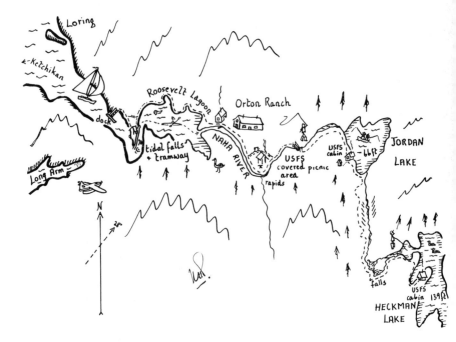

end of the lagoon. Beware of mice and squirrels. Hang up your food! Black bear may also visit this area during salmon migrations upriver.

The trail upriver, across a suspension bridge to Jordan Lake, is good, but it becomes boggy as it approaches Heckman Lake. The path follows the shoreline of Jordan Lake past the USFS cabin, then climbs onto a side hill above the creek. About 0.5 mile from Heckman Lake is a magical world of river rapids, pools, moss-covered rocks, and a waterfall where steelhead lurk. A walk by dark, still pools, part of Heckman Lake, ends at the second USFS cabin placed above a bay of the lake. Both cabins are in good condition. Register with the USFS before going. Please clean up and take out all garbage and unused food to discourage bears and little creatures.

Some people walk a tagged route from Heckman Lake to Harriet Hunt Lake (at the north end of the Ward Lake road system). This route is not easy to find and should only be attempted with a local who is familiar with the country.

*Naha River at Orton Ranch*

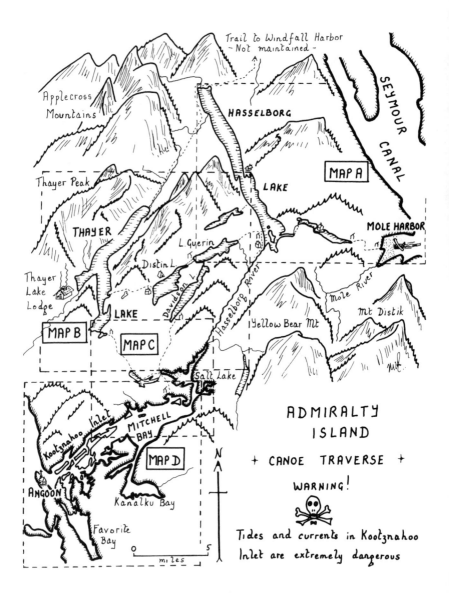

Trail to Windfall Harbor
~Not maintained~

Applecross Mountains

HASSELBORG

SEYMOUR CANAL

MAP A

LAKE

Thayer Peak

MOLE HARBOR

THAYER

L. Guerin

Distin L.

Thayer Lake Lodge

Davidson

Hasselborg River

Mole River

Mt Distik

LAKE

MAP B

MAP C

Yellow Bear Mt

Salt Lake

ADMIRALTY ISLAND

Mitchell Bay

Kootznahoo Inlet

MAP D

N

+ CANOE TRAVERSE +

WARNING!

ANGOON

Kanalku Bay

Tides and currents in Kootznahoo Inlet are extremely dangerous

Favorite Bay

0                    5
miles

# ADMIRALTY ISLAND

## A1
## ADMIRALTY ISLAND CANOE TRAVERSE

**TIME:** 4–6 days
**DISTANCE:** 32 miles
**RATING:** strenuous
**ACCESS:** floatplane, or ferry to Angoon; 50 air miles south of Juneau
**TYPE:** fresh and saltwater lagoons, forest
**MAPS:** Sitka C-1; C-2; and B-2, 1:63,360
Take Juneau tide tables and collapsible water carriers
USFS cabins and shelters
Beware of dangerous tidal currents east of Angoon

Admiralty Island is Kootznoowoo, Fortress of the Brown Bear, and, with the highest concentration of brown bears anywhere, is accurately named. It is also home to the bald eagle, Sitka black-tailed deer, pine marten, nuthatch, and huge trees in climax forests with floors carpeted with moss. Much of it is now national monument and wilderness despite continuing pressures to log and mine.

A little south of the geographic center of the island, a sprinkling of lakes is strung like a diamond bracelet, connecting Mole Harbor with Mitchell Bay through a natural break in the mountainous backbone. Trails connect the lakes with each other and with the tidewater bays, and Angoon is the western gateway to one of the most picturesque wilderness backwaters in Southeast Alaska, Mitchell Bay.

In summer a ferry calls in Angoon at least twice a week from Sitka and Juneau. Also canoeists can charter a floatplane out of Juneau, Petersburg, or Sitka and fly directly to tidewater or to any of the larger lakes. Experienced canoeists may find the 3- to 4-day paddle trip from Juneau to Mole Harbor an exciting challenge. This extended trip is described after the main Mole Harbor to Angoon trip.

Three-sided shelters built by the CCC in the 1930s remain at strategic spots. They make good overnight accommodations for those who can live with the wildlife—mosquitos, no-see-ums, white socks, mink, marten, playful otters, yodeling loons and curious bears. Beware of mink, marten, and voles; they steal food if given the chance. No permit is required, and shelters are open to all comers at all times. Please use a cooking stove or replenish the wood supply before leaving. Stack it in a dry place. Hang food in a tree at least 12 feet from the ground, 100 feet away from camp. Cabins are available and more comfortable, but they isolate campers from the excitement outside. Register with the USFS for an overnight cabin stay. Refer to the address given in appendix C.

If there is time, do not miss Thayer Lake, a lodge built and operated by the Nelson family, situated on the Thayer Creek outlet. Bob built his own overshot waterwheel, and he has a unique system of regulating the water flow to give continuous electricity. It makes for a quiet operation, in which the falling water blends with other environmental sounds.

Mitchell Bay, Kanalku Bay, and Favorite Bay are under joint management of the USFS and Angoon village corporation (Kootznoowoo Inc.). Visitors are welcomed by the Native people and Admiralty Island National Monument, but they are asked to respect the cultural heritage and rights of the local people of Angoon. Camp only in designated campsites. A list of these is available at Centennial Hall in Juneau. Some are mentioned in the text. Kootznahoo Inlet, the narrow entrance that connects Mitchell Bay with Angoon, can be run on a 13-foot tide or less with relative safety. The best time is shortly before and after high slack. Avoid half tides and low low tides, when water turbulence is extreme and rocks uncovered. Add 2 hours to the Juneau tide tables for Mitchell Bay tides. Canoes are rented by Alaska Discovery in Angoon and Juneau.

Use maps Sitka C-1; C-2; and B-2, 1:63,360 for the island traverse. For an overall view of the area, Sitka and Sumdum 1:250,000 are useful. If desired, nautical charts for tidal areas may be included: 1:20,000 Mole and Windfall Harbors No. 8228 and 1:30,000 Kootznahoo Inlet No. 8247. The Admiralty Island National Monument (USFS) has printed an informational map for the section between Mole Harbor and Angoon. It is compact enough to take along as a handy reference.

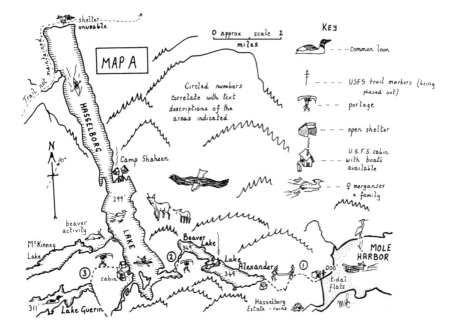

KEY

- - - Common loon

$\dagger$ - - - - USFS trail markers (being phased out)

- - - portage

- - - open shelter

- - - U.S.F.S cabin with boats available

- - - ♀ merganser + family

MAP A

*Circled numbers correlate with text descriptions of the areas indicated.*

O approx scale 2 miles

shelter unusable

Trail not maintained

HASSELBORG

N 30°

Camp Shaheen

299'

beaver activity

McKinney Lake

LAKE

③ cabin

311' Lake Guerin

Beaver Lake 349'

② Lake Alexander 349'

① 000'

tidal flats

Hasselborg Estate - ruins

MOLE HARBOR

# MOLE HARBOR TO HASSELBORG LAKE

**TIME:** 1—2 days
**DISTANCE:** 9—13 miles
4 cabins, 3 shelters available
The bracketed numbers below correspond to the circled numbers on the maps.

Whatever the mode of travel to Mole Harbor, plan to arrive at high tide to facilitate unloading. A large portion of the bay is mud flat at low tide.

A three-sided, wood-roofed shelter is just visible, 1 mile north of Mole River at the west end of the bay. The portage trail to Lake Alexander starts from this point. Watch for Arctic loon as well as common and red-throated loon in the bay, plus kittiwakes and Bonaparte's gulls farther north. The harbor itself also teems with sandpipers, yellowlegs, herons, and more. Please respect the rights of private land owners adjacent to the trail corridor and Mole River. A field of fireweed by the river was the site of Hasselborg's tiny cabin, now a pile of boards lying flat on the moss. In late summer, watch for bears catching humpback salmon on the same river flats. Deer may be seen on the beach.

A 2.5-mile portage connects the tidal harbor to Lake Alexander

[1]. After climbing to about 600 feet above sea level, the trail gently drops to the lake where there is a CCC shelter in good condition. Estimate about 1-mile-per-hour for a portage, if just one trip is made. The time is more than doubled when boats are carried separately from gear. The paddle to the USFS cabin from the shelter is 1.7 miles and takes about 40 minutes. From the cabin, paddle quietly through a lily-covered slough that winds west, then north, before emerging into Beaver Lake. Many species of ducks and geese may be using the lily pads as cover; also loons and red-tailed hawks haunt the general area.

A small opening on the south shore, about 200 yards before the end of Beaver Lake, points the way to the next portage. The passage is almost 0.5 mile long and ends in tall grass and rushes. The Beaver Lake outflow cascades from here to Lake Hasselborg. The 0.3 mile portage is not difficult [2]. Total distance from the Lake Alexander cabin is 2.3 miles. Paddling distance from here to the next portage, with a CCC shelter, is 1.8 miles. The USFS Hasselborg River Cabin is close by and roughly the same distance. Paddling distance to Camp Shaheen (two USFS cabins) is 4 miles. (The mileages quoted are point-to-point distances.)

Hasselborg Lake, roughly 9 miles long, is ringed by shapely peaks at its northern end. Hasselborg Creek flows out to Mitchell Bay at the southwest extremity, close to the Hasselborg River cabin. A fishing trail goes from this cabin and follows the river downstream over a series of waterfalls. Also a boardwalk, 0.3 mile long, connects the river cabin to the Lake Guerin portage trail [3] and CCC shelter, which is in good condition, with a wooden floor.

Camp Shaheen lies on the east shore of Lake Hasselborg, about halfway up the lake. Another campsite sits on a graveled spit close to a stream at the north end of the lake, but don't bother with the shelter. It is standing in a beaver pond and is unusable. A trail connecting Windfall Harbor with Hasselborg and Thayer lakes has not been brushed for years and is very hard to find. Another angler's trail, a rather pleasant one, connects Hasselborg Lake with McKinney Lake. It is almost 1 mile long and starts on the west shore, opposite from Camp Shaheen. A large camping area is located in the trees close to a stream and the beginning of the trail. The path ascends about 150 feet, then drops about 50 feet to McKinney Lake, where a boat is stowed on the shore.

Many loons and mergansers make this area their home. Listen for the yodeling of the common loon and the banshee wails of the red-throated loon. Both species are shy of noisy people. Do not try to approach too closely.

# GUERIN, DISTIN AND DAVIDSON LAKES

**TIME:** 2 days
**DISTANCE:** Hasselborg Lake to Salt Lake 9.6 to 10.8 miles, depending on
route
Two cabins, two shelters available

When approaching the portage to Lake Guerin from Hasselborg
Lake, look for the CCC shelter. A diamond marker may be visible from
the west end, but the USFS has virtually eliminated all diamond mark-

*Three-sided shelter at Lake Guerin*

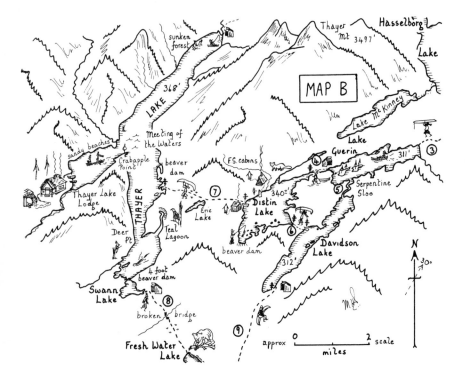

ers because they are not suitable for wilderness. The 1.7 mile trail is mostly boardwalk [3] with a staircase on the east end. Take care on wet boards. The paddle down Lake Guerin to the CCC shelter at the west end is 2.3 miles, about 70 minutes. The shelter keeps the rain out, but heavy use has created a mud puddle in front and the floor is wet dirt. The place is pretty, however. Yellow Bear Mountain, Botany Peak, and Mount Distik dominate the skyline to the southeast, and a quiet, sheltered stretch of lake with lily pads reaches almost to the shelter.

The portage to Distin Lake, upstream from the shelter, is short (0.4 mile) and not difficult [4]. The rise is about 30 feet (the topo map cannot be correct, with a 1-foot difference between lakes). When it is high, the river can be run from west to east, but check for windfalls first. If trees have fallen across the creek, they can be very dangerous. The portage is marked on the west side, and the approach is once more a lily-choked lagoon. There are two USFS cabins on Distin Lake; one, built by the Territorial Sportsmen of Juneau, 1.4 miles from the portage; the other, a shelter converted to a primitive cabin, 2.2 miles from the portage. Both are on the northwest shoreline. The Thayer Lake Trail [7] starts from the latter, more southerly, cabin. Cutthroat and Dolly Varden trout fishing is generally good in front of a beaver dam at the southernmost point of Distin Lake.

Another short portage (0.3 mile) joins Distin and Davidson lakes [6]. Well-marked at both ends, the trail is boardwalk and runs through open pine country with views of Distin Lake and Thayer Mountain. Davidson Lake can be reached from Lake Guerin through a charming snakelike backwater [5], which attracts varied species of waterfowl. The passageway on the south shore, south of two islands, may be overlooked at first because of tall grass, tall trees, and a sharp bend to the right. The boats may have to be lifted over a gravel bar about a foot high against a gentle current (indicating that it is Davidson that is a foot higher than Guerin, not Distin as shown on the topographic map). Paddle in silence around the corners so as not to disturb any grazing deer or other wildlife.

Davidson Lake is 3.6 miles long and has a CCC shelter at the southern end, where the trail to Mitchell Bay begins [9]. Those in a hurry take this route for the shortest way through the lake system. This portage is tough, 2.4 miles to Salt Lake in the upper reaches of Mitchell Bay. The path climbs 200 feet above Davidson Lake, then drops gently to tidewater through small trees. Turn left at the first trail junction to launch the boats into Salt Lake. To reach the trail leading to a three-sided shelter in Mitchell Bay [12], turn right, then left across the bridge between Fresh Water and Salt lakes.

# THAYER LAKE

**TIME:** 1–2 days
**SHORTEST DISTANCE:** Distin to Fresh Water Lake; 7.7 miles
Two shelters available

The trail to Thayer Lake starts by the smaller, more southerly, cabin on Distin Lake and goes by a good fishing lake, locally called Erik Lake. The trail is 3 miles long, in fair shape, and climbs about 400 feet in both directions over hills and through swales (the route marked on the USGS map is not correct). It is a beautiful trail through old-growth forest. On the west end, an opening gives views of the ridge above and glimpses through trees of Thayer Lake, but the route is wet. Those going eastward, look for a USFS marker on the shore, 1.3 miles southeast of Crabapple Point.

Thayer Lake is Y shaped: the south arm to a beaver dam and Swan Lake is 3.3 miles; the southwest arm to Thayer Lake Lodge and Thayer

Creek is 1.8 miles; and the north arm to a CCC shelter is 4 miles long
and ringed by shapely mountains. Shallow areas are marked by home-
made buoys, but watch for snags in the water. Some are seeded with lichens, mosses, tall grasses, ferns, and small flowers, and some are even
nesting habitat for mew gulls, presumably to escape land predators.
Others don't quite break the surface and are a hazard to boats. Look
into the dark brown waters, especially of the north arm, to see forests
of sunken deadfalls. The south arm has camping spots behind sandy
beaches and tall pine trees, and the shoreline is a riot of flowers in
midsummer. Lake fishing is found close to rivers and streams, and pan-
size cutthroat and Dolly Varden trout are abundant.

The beaver dam on the southern toe of the south arm is at least 5
feet high, and boats have to be pulled over and relaunched into Swan
Lake. The lake is about 0.5 mile long, and it ends with tall grass, mud,
and a deep boghole to jump across. The shelter immediately behind
the boghole is in good condition. The 2.2-mile trail to Fresh Water
Lake [8] has been relocated to Lake Edith (unnamed on the topo map).

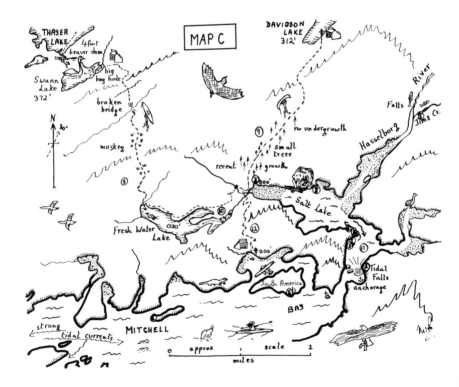

Small hills amount to about 100 feet of climbing southbound, and one climbs at least 400 feet going north. New raw trail, in parts, is hilly and makes going difficult. A stream is found under a grove of large trees where the trail first meets Fresh Water Lake.

# FRESH WATER AND SALT LAKES

**TIME:** 75-minute walk from west end of Fresh Water Lake to Mitchell
    Bay shelter. 3–4 ± hours paddling, depending on tides
**DISTANCE:** land, 3 miles; water, 7 miles
Beware of tidal falls
One shelter available
Check map for designated campsites
    Fresh Water Lake can be paddled almost to the bridge, although the east end is a battle of grass, and there is a partially submerged log that has to be climbed over when waters are low [10]. Follow the current and watch for grass bent over by previous boats. Try to ignore the no-see-ums. The bridge will appear immediately after the towel has been thrown in! The Thayer Lake Trail is not visible, but it is within a stone's throw on the north shore. It is doubtful that boats can be floated under the bridge because the stream is choked with windfalls, but if it is open, bear in mind that headroom is only a few inches.
    An alternative is to follow the the Thayer Lake Trail as it continues along the northern shore of Fresh Water Lake, 1.9 miles. It meets the Davidson Lake trail at the first of two Y junctions. Turn right (south) to reach the Mitchell Bay CCC shelter [12] overland. Go left, then bear right, to get to Salt Lake and a large campsite under big spruce trees. Turn left at the second Y junction to return to Davidson Lake. Biting flies, including clegs or deerfly, can be numerous and voracious in this area. Those walking to the shelter should cross the Fresh Water Lake outflow, then walk about 1 mile over a 100 foot hill to a tidal bay behind South America Island.
    It is best to launch into Salt Lake at high tide. Windfalls and shallow water usually prevent river-running the couple of hundred yards to the grass flats. Boats can be portaged to the campsite at Salt Lake and then carried across the grass meadow. But if the tide is low, boats must be hauled through mud. A paddle through the dark quiet backwaters, overshadowed by huge trees that form the skyline in places in Salt Lake, makes a heady interlude after the strenuous boat and gear hauling. Consult the map for campsites. The island sites, both without water, in upper and lower Salt Lakes are most recommended for pri-

vacy. Approach the Tidal Falls with caution [11]. At most stages of the tide, they form whitewater falls, but kayakers can pull out on the east bank and line down without difficulty.

## MITCHELL BAY

**TIME:** 1–2 days

Mitchell Bay is a collection of tidal islands, inlets, backwaters, and tidal falls. Trumpeter swans winter here, seals and sea lion frequent the area, geese in their hundreds use the tidal flats for feeding, murrelets and herons are seen almost anywhere, and ravens hurl obscenities

*Local children at Mitchell Bay*

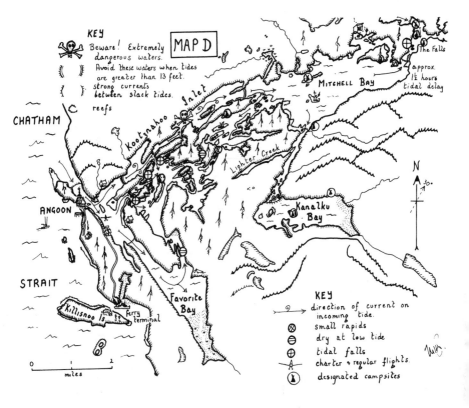

KEY
☠ Beware! Extremely dangerous waters.
)( Avoid these waters when tides are greater than 13 feet.
{ } strong currents between slack tides.
～ reefs

MAP D

CHATHAM

Kootznahoo Inlet

MITCHELL BAY

The Falls

approx. 1½ hours tidal delay

Lighter Creek

ANGOON

Kanalku Bay

N

STRAIT

Favorite Bay

Killisnoo Is.

ferry terminal

0    1    2
miles

KEY
→ direction of current on incoming tide.
⊗ small rapids
⊖ dry at low tide
⊕ tidal falls
✈ charter & regular flights
① designated campsites

at passing travelers close to the village of Angoon. Tide table, map and compass, common sense, and a sensitivity towards the local villagers and their ancient heritage are essential for passage. Camping is allowed on 14 designated sites, some of which have no water.

About 0.5 mile south of the Tidal Falls, Mitchell Bay opens up to the west, and Kluchman Rock (with a small memorial to a fatal boating incident years ago) is visible to the right. Go around the rock and head north to reach the CCC shelter and trail end. The run from Salt Lake is about 5 miles and takes about 3 hours, depending on the tide. Camping is also found on the south shore of South America Island and Diamond Island. Carry water.

Kanalku Bay is another interesting paddle that is dependent on tide conditions, and requires the same precautions as noted elsewhere. A campsite is located on the east shore at the northern entrance to Davis Creek, and another dry camp is found on a burned island in the south-center of Kanalku Bay (see map).

Timing is of the essence when planning to run Kootznahoo Inlet. Paddle out of Mitchell Bay when high tide starts to turn, but only go through the main channel on a tide of 13 feet or less. Those going into Mitchell Bay should start at low slack (quiet waters at the tidal change) on an average tide. If necessary, wait for sufficient water. Be sure the tide is right before entering and be prepared to pull onto shore if the current is too fast or dangerous. Allow two hours to paddle from the shelter to Hemlock Point, almost 4 miles, and another two hours to arrive in Angoon, a little over 5 miles.

A longer and fun route weaves through the back channels. Here quiet backwaters teem with life, and some of the passageways are so narrow they cannot be seen until entered. The trees almost touch overhead. In many places, unruffled lagoons open directly to the main channel and are linked by rapids or tidal falls, depending on the tide at the time. Sometimes it is fun to wait out a tide and watch the whitewater build up in the narrow passageways and main channel. This is where a map or chart and compass is useful. See the map for two dry, primitive campsites in the back passages between Mitchell Bay and Angoon.

Exit Mitchell Bay through the back channels to about the halfway point on an incoming (flood) tide. The outgoing (ebb) tide flushes boats out to Angoon. Those going in the opposite direction must negotiate a way into Favorite Bay and the westernmost bays on an incoming tide, then wait for the ebb to paddle into Mitchell Bay. Beware of tidal falls and rapids.

Groceries can be obtained at the Angoon Trading Company, about 1 mile south of town. The ferry dock is 2.5 miles south of Angoon, opposite Killisnoo Island on Chatham Strait. Camping is not available in Angoon, but there are lodges and a bed and breakfast.

# JUNEAU TO MOLE HARBOR

**TIME:** 3–5 days
**DISTANCE:** 55 miles
**RATING:** strenuous
**MAPS:** Juneau A-1; B-1; Sitka D-1, 1:63,360; and Juneau and Sitka
1:250,000 for an overall view. See the introduction for chart in-
formation.
**REQUIREMENTS:** sea kayaking experience; Juneau tide tables; USFS
permit to land at Pack Creek

For experienced kayakers, this is a rewarding paddle and saves on
the air charter fare to Mole Harbor! The backwaters of Seymour Canal
are very lovely and full of wildlife. A tramway at Oliver Inlet, rebuilt by
the Juneau Volunteers and the National Guard in 1984, connects Stephens Passage with Seymour Canal and facilitates portaging to a state
maintained cabin on the northern end of the canal, 17 miles south of
Juneau. Apply to the State Division of Parks to use the cabin.

A USFS permit is required to land at Pack Creek, 30 miles south of
Juneau, where bears are seen on the creek or shoreline almost every
day in July and August. **Do not camp in the area.** If taking food, put it
in the cache provided. The permit and information on regulations can
be obtained at the USFS Information Center, Centennial Hall in Juneau.

Note: Allow extra days to wait out bad weather situations for the
passage down Gastineau Channel, across Stephens Passage, and parts
of Seymour Canal. Wear a life jacket.

The start can be made from Sandy Beach in Douglas or at Thane,
3.8 miles south of Juneau. Paddle south down Gastineau Channel to
Marmion Island and Tantallion Point. Behind Marmion Island there is a
headland and beach that makes a good picnic lunch spot. From here
2.5 miles of open water separate Douglas Island from Admiralty Island.
Do not cross in rough conditions.

The crossing to Oliver Inlet, 4.5 miles southwest of Marmion Island, takes about 1.5 hours, and the paddle to the portage on the
southwest shore of Oliver Inlet (2.8 miles) takes about 45 minutes, depending on the state of tide. Arrange to go into the inlet up to 3 hours
before high slack to give a chance to ride the current in and load the
boats onto the tramway dolly. On average tides it is possible to go into
the entrance during low slack. If in doubt walk the entrance first to
check for whitewater.

Allow at least 2 hours to portage boats and gear the mile to the
cabin. Please grease the dolly wheels; grease is available by the winch

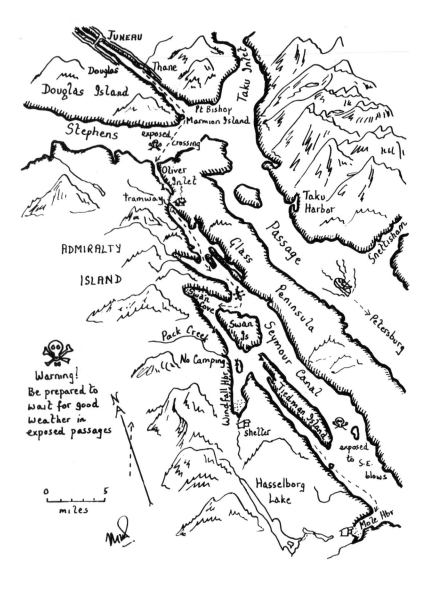

JUNEAU

Douglas

Thane

Douglas Island

Stephens

Pt Bishop

Marmion Island

exposed

Crossing

Oliver Inlet

tramway

Taku Inlet

Taku Harbor

Passage

Snettisham

ADMIRALTY

ISLAND

Glass

Peninsula

Swan Cove

Swan Is

Seymour Canal

Petersburg

Pack Creek

No Camping

Windfall Hbr

Tiedman Island

shelter

exposed
to S.E.
blows

Warning!
Be prepared to
wait for good
weather in
exposed passages

N

Hasselborg
Lake

Mole Hbr

0        5
mi les

on the north end. Be careful; the brakes will not stop the tram cart fully on a hill. Leave the cart above the high tide mark. The cabin is located at the south end of the portage. Good camping is also found on the west shore of Oliver Inlet about a quarter of a mile north of the portage. In camp, always hang the food in a tree, away from tents and boats.

The first mile at the northern end of Seymour Canal is mud at low tide, and a 15-foot tide is needed to float a small boat in the slough by the cabin. Those wishing to float kayaks into the bay without waiting for the tide can portage to a stream on the west side.

Follow the west coastline past a waterfall, a good source of water and campsite, to Windfall Harbor. At the head of the bay a three-sided shelter in good condition offers pleasant camping. Salmon fishing is good in the area. There is a trail to Hasselborg Lake, but it has not been brushed for years and is hard to find. At the north end of the harbor is Pack Creek, where visitation is limited to the daytime hours (9:00 A.M. to 9:00 P.M.). A planked trail, almost 1 mile long, leads to a bear observatory upriver. Walk the beach south about 0.5 mile to find the trail to the left of a small feeder stream. It is more likely, however, that bears will be seen on the tidal flats and are too habituated to humans for comfort. If a stay is planned, camp on Swan Island, on the north end of Tiedeman Island; on Windfall Island, at the head of the bay; or 3 miles north of Pack Creek, on a headland on the Admiralty shoreline.

The distance to Windfall Island from the Seymour Canal Cabin is 17 miles, and from there to Mole Harbor another 21 miles. (This does not include side explorations into interesting bays and inlets.) Mole Harbor is overshadowed by the graceful lines of Mount Distik, 3,801 feet to the southwest. It also has about a mile of mud at low tide.

# APPENDICES

## A. Recommended reading and reference material

### MOUNTAINEERING AND BACKPACKING

Lentz, Martha. *Mountaineering First Aid,* Seattle: The Mountaineers, 1985.

Manning, Harvey. *Backpacking: One Step at a Time,* Seattle: REI Press, 1972.

Peters, Ed, ed. *Mountaineering: The Freedom of the Hills,* Seattle: The Mountaineers, 1982.

### FLORA AND FAUNA

Armstrong, Robert. *A Guide to the Birds of Alaska,* Bothell, Washington: Alaska Northwest Books, 1983.

Carl, George Clifford. *Guide to Marine Life of British Columbia,* British Columbia Provincial Museum. Handbook No. 21, 1978.

Dufresne, Frank. *Alaska's Animals and Fishes,* New York: A. S. Barnes and Co., 1946.

*Heller, Christine. *Wild, Edible and Poisonous Plants of Alaska,* University of Alaska, Co-operative Extension Services.

*Islieb, Pete, et al. *Birds of Southeast Alaska: A checklist,* Alaska Natural History Association, 1987.

Miller, Jr., Orson K. *Mushrooms of North America,* New York: Chanticleer Press, 1984.

Ricketts, Edward R., and Calvin, Jack. *Between Pacific Tides,* Stanford, California: Stanford University Press, 1952.

*Robuck, Wayne. *Common Alpine Plants of Southeast Alaska,* Portland, Oregon: Pacific Northwest Research Station.

*————. *Common Forest Plants of Southeast Alaska,* Portland, Oregon: Pacific Northwest Research Station.

*————. *Common Muskeg Plants of Southeast Alaska,* Portland, Oregon: Pacific Northwest Research Station.

Sharples, Ada White. *Alaska Wild Flowers,* Stanford, California: Stanford University Press, 1938.

*Stromsen, Nancy E. *A Guide to Alaskan Seabirds,* Alaska Natural History Association in cooperation with the Fish and Wildlife Service, U.S. Department of the Interior.

## GEOLOGY

Connor, Cathy. *Roadside Geology of Alaska,* Missoula, Montana: Mountain Press, 1988.

## HISTORY

Berton, Pierre. *Klondike Fever,* New York: Alfred Knopf, 1958.

Chevigny, Hector. *Lord of Alaska,* Portland, Oregon: Binfords and Mort, 1951.

DeArmond, R. N. *Some Names Around Juneau,* Sitka, Alaska: Sitka Printing, 1957.

Morgan, Murray. *One Man's Gold Rush,* Seattle: University of Washington Press, 1967.

## GENERAL

Dufresne, Frank. *No Room for Bears,* New York: Holt, Rinehart and Winston, 1965.

Muir, John. *Travels in Alaska,* New York, Houghton Mifflin, 1915 (out of print).

* *Indicates pamphlet*

# B. Bibliography

## FLORA AND FAUNA

Heller, Christine. *Wild Flowers of Alaska,* Portland, Oregon: Graphic Arts Center, 1966.

*Muller, Mary Clay. *A Preliminary Checklist of the Vascular Plants in Southeastern Alaska,* USDA Forest Service, Alaska Region.

National Geographic. *A Field Guide to the Birds of North America,* Washington, D.C.: National Geographic Society, 1987.

Robbins, Chandler S., et al. *Birds of North America,* New York: Golden Press, Western Publishing, 1966.

*Viereck, Leslie A., et al. *Guide to Alaska Trees,* Washington D.C.: USDA Forest Service, 1974.

*Weeden, Robert B., and Ellison, Laurence N. *Upland Game Birds of Forest and Tundra,* Alaska Department of Fish and Game, Wildlife Booklet Series: No. 3, Dec. 1968.

White, Helen A., ed. *The Alaska-Yukon Wild Flowers Guide,* Anchorage, Alaska: Alaska Northwest Publishing Company, 1974.

## TRAILS

*Janes, Willette. *In the Miners' Footsteps,* Juneau, Alaska: Juneau-Douglas City Museum, Parks and Recreation Department, 1985.

King, Mary Lou. *90 Short Walks Around Juneau,* Juneau, Alaska: Taku Conservation Society, Juneau Audubon Society, 1988.

*USDA Forest Service. *Juneau Trails,* Tongass National Forest, Juneau Ranger District.

*USDA Forest Service. *Sitka Trails,* Tongass National Forest, Sitka Ranger District.

Also various USFS, Canadian National Parks, NPS, and Alaska Department of Environment conservation pamphlets on bears, giardiasis, and hypothermia; and Chuck's Camera.

*\* Indicates pamphlet*

# C. Addresses and telephone numbers

Telephone prefix (area code) for entire state of Alaska is 907.

## STATE OF ALASKA

### Fishing and hunting licenses:
Alaska Department of Revenue, Fish and Game Licensing Section
111 West 8th Street, Juneau, AK 99801 (465-2376)

### Fish and game information:
Alaska Department of Fish and Game, Public Communications Section,
P.O. Box 3-2000, Juneau, AK 99801 (465-4113)

Department of Fish and Game, Division of Sports Fish (local offices):
Haines and Skagway Office: P.O. Box 330, Haines, AK 99827 (766-
    2625)
Juneau Office: P.O. Box 20, Douglas, AK 99824 (465-4270)
Ketchikan Office: 2030 Sealevel Drive, Suite 205, Ketchikan, AK
    99901 (225-2859)
Petersburg Office: P.O. Box 667, Petersburg, AK 99833 (772-3801)
Sitka Office: 304 Lake Street, Room 103, Sitka, AK 99835 (747-6688)
Wrangell Office: P.O. Box 200, Wrangell, AK 99929 (874-3822)

Co-operative Extension Service, USDA, University of Alaska, Fairbanks,
    AK 99775

# BED AND BREAKFAST

Alaska Bed and Breakfast Association—Southeastern Alaska,
    P.O. Box 3-6500, Suite 169, Juneau, AK 99802 (586-2959)

These people will make reservations in the following communities:
    Skagway, Haines, Gustavus, Elfin Cove, Pelican, Juneau,
    Angoon, Sitka, and Petersburg.

# CHILKOOT TRAIL

Department of Indian Affairs and Northern Development,
    P.O. Box 1767, Whitehorse, Yukon Y1A 544
Chilkoot Boat Tours, RR3 #1, Site 20, Comp. 34, Whitehorse, Yukon
    Y1A 426 (403-668-7766)
Canadian Park Service, Chilkoot Trail National Historic Park, P.O. Box
    5540, Whitehorse, Yukon Y1A 544 (403-668-2116)
Canada Customs, Whitehorse, (403-667-6471)
Fraser, (403-821-4111)
Royal Canadian Mounted Police, Whitehorse, Yukon Y1A
    (403-667-5555)
U.S. Customs, Skagway, AK 99840 (907-983-2325)
U.S. NPS, Klondike Gold Rush Historical Park, P.O. Box 517, Skagway,
    AK 99840 (907-983-2921)
White Pass and Yukon Route, P.O. Box 435, Skagway, AK 99840 (1-
    800-343-7373 or 907-983-2217)

# ADMIRALTY ISLAND

Admiralty National Monument, P.O. Box 2097, Juneau, AK 99802
    (789-3111)
Alaska Discovery, Inc., 369 South Franklin, Juneau, AK 99801 (586-
    1911)
Alaska Discovery, Inc., c/o Angoon Trading Company, K. J. Metcalf,
    Angoon Rep., P.O. Box 10, Angoon, AK 99820 (788-3111)

State of Alaska, Department of Natural Resources, Division of Parks and
    Recreation, 400 Willoughby, Juneau, AK 99801 (465-4563)
    (For Oliver Inlet tramway information and cabin reservations.)
Thayer Lake Lodge, winter address: P.O. Box 5416, Ketchikan, AK
    99901 (225-3343) or P.O. Box 211614, Auke Bay, AK 99821
    (789-5646); summer phone: 789-0944 (Juneau) or 225-6371
    (Ketchikan)

## JUNEAU

City/Borough of Juneau, Parks and Recreation Department, 155 South
    Seward Street, Juneau, AK 99801 (586-5226). Call for hike
    schedule; recording after office hours. See "U.S. Forest Service"
    for cabin and trail information.

## PETERSBURG

Petersburg Youth Program, P.O. Box 842, Petersburg, AK 99833 (772-
    4422)

## SITKA

Sitka National Historical Park, P.O. Box 738, Sitka, AK 99835 (747-
    6281)
Alaska Raptor Rehabilitation Center, P.O. Box 2984, Sitka, AK 99835
    (747-8662)

## TOPOGRAPHIC MAPS

U.S. Geological Survey, P.O. Box 25286, Federal Center, Denver, CO
    80255 or New Federal Building, Box 12, 101 12th Avenue,
    Fairbanks, AK 99701

## CHARTS

NOAA/National Ocean Service, 222 West 7th Avenue, #38,
    Anchorage, AK 99513
NOAA/National Ocean Service, 1801 Fairview Avenue East, Seattle,
    WA 98102

## U.S. FOREST SERVICE

Central location for cabin reservations and general information on the
    Tongass National Forest, including Admiralty National
    Monument: USFS Information Center, Centennial Hall, 101
    Egan Drive, Juneau, AK 99801 (586-8751)
Juneau Ranger District: 8465 Old Dairy Road, Juneau, AK 99801
    (789-3111)

Ketchikan Ranger District: 3031 Tongass, Ketchikan, AK 99901 (225-2148)
Petersburg Ranger District: P.O. Box 1328, Petersburg, AK 99833 (772-3871)
Sitka Ranger District: 204 Siginaka Way, Sitka, AK 99835 (747-6671)
Stikine Area Supervisor's Office: P.O. Box 309, Petersburg, AK 99833 (772-3841)
Wrangell Ranger District: P.O. Box 51, Wrangell, AK 99929 (874-2323)

## YOUTH HOSTELS

AYH, P.O. Box 37613, Washington, D.C. 20013 (202-783-6161)
Bear Creek Camp and Hostel, Box 1158, Haines, AK 99827. Location: Small Tract Road, 2 miles south of Haines; open all year. (766-2259)
Juneau International Hostel, 614 Harris Street, Juneau, AK 99801. Location: four blocks from downtown; open all year. (586-9559)
Ketchikan Youth Hostel, P.O. Box 8515, Ketchikan, AK 99901. Location: United Methodist Church (UMC); open June 1 to September 1. (225-3319)
Sitka Youth Hostel, P.O. Box 2645, Sitka, AK 99835. Location: UMC, Edgecumbe and Kimshan streets; open June 1 to September 1. (747-8356)

## CONSERVATION COUNCIL

Southeast Alaskan Conservation Council (SEACC), P.O. Box 021692, Juneau, AK 99802 (586-6942)

# D. Index of Trails

## SHORT WALKS

Walks close to ferry, tour ships, and airport (in Juneau) for those with limited time.

**Haines**
> H2 Mount Riley (Battery Point Trail)

**Juneau**
> J1 Mount Roberts (first viewpoint)
> J2 Perseverance
> J13 Mendenhall Wetlands

**Sitka**
> St4 Totem Walk

**Skagway**
> S2 Lower Dewey Lake
> S5 Yakutania Point
> S6 Gold Rush Cemetery

**Wrangell**
> W1 Wrangell City Walk

## DAY HIKES

From tour ship, ferry, or town without other transportation.

**Haines**
> H1 Mount Ripinsky
> H2 Mount Riley

**Juneau**
> J1 Mount Roberts
> J3 Mount Juneau
> J4 Granite Creek Basin
> J5 Dan Moller Ski Trail

**Ketchikan**
> K1 Deer Mountain

**Petersburg**
> P1 Raven's Roost

**Sitka**
> St1 Gavan Hill
> St3 Mount Verstovia
> St5 Indian River

**Skagway**
> S3 Upper Dewey Lake
> S4 Magic Forest
> S7 Skyline Trail and A. B. Mountain
> S8 Denver Glacier

## ROUTES REQUIRING TRANSPORTATION FROM TOWN

Unless otherwise marked, transportation is by car or bicycle.

**Haines**
> H1 Mount Ripinsky (to Seven Mile Saddle)
> H2 Mount Riley
> H3 Seduction Point

**Juneau**
> J6 Mount Jumbo
> J7 Treadwell Ditch (two cars)
> J8 Sheep Creek
> J9 Bishop Point
> J10 Salmon Creek
> J11 Blackerby Ridge
> J14 East Glacier Complex
> J15 Nugget Creek
> J16 Thunder Mountain
> J17 West Glacier and Mount McGinnis
> J18 Auke Nu and Spaulding Meadows
> J19 Peterson Lake
> J20 Montana Creek (two cars)
> J21 Windfall Lake
> J22 Herbert Glacier
> J23 Amalga-Eagle Glacier
> J24 Yankee Basin

J25 Point Bridget and
Bridget Cove

**Ketchikan**

K2 Mahoney Mountain
K3 Twin Peaks
K4 Ward Lake
K5 Perseverance Lake
K6 Connell Lake and
Brown Mountain
K7 Wolf Lakes (boat and
car)
K8 Naha (boat)

**Petersburg**

P2 Petersburg Mountain
P3 Petersburg Creek
(boat)

**Sitka**

St2 Harbor Mountain
St6 Beaver Lake
St7 Airport Causeway
(boat)

**Skagway**

S1 Chilkoot Trail
S9 Laughton Glacier
S10 Lost Lake

**Wrangell**

W2 Rainbow Falls

# CANOE WILDERNESS

**Admiralty Island**

A1 Admiralty Island Canoe
Traverse

# WINTER TRAILS

**Juneau**

J5 Dan Moller Ski Trail
(cabin)
J7 Treadwell Ditch (ice
fishing)
J17 West Glacier
J18 Auke Nu and
Spaulding Meadows
(cabin)

J19 Peterson Lake (cabin,
ice fishing, and skiing)
J20 Montana Creek
J21 Windfall Lake (ice
fishing)
J22 Herbert Glacier
J23 Amalga-Eagle Glacier
J25 Point Bridget

**Ketchikan**

K4 Ward Lake (skating)

**Petersburg**

P1 Raven's Roost
(intermediate alpine
skiing)

**Sitka**

St5 Indian River

**Skagway**

S1 Chilkoot Trail (skiing,
Dyea to Canyon City;
skiing, Log Cabin to
Bennett; skiing, Log Cabin
to Lindeman)
S2 Lower Dewey Lake (ice
fishing and skating)
S7 Skyline Trail
S9 Laughton Glacier

# TRAILS TO BE AVOIDED IN WINTER AND LATE SPRING

All trails classified "alpine" or
"strenuous," unless experienced
in winter mountaineering.

**Juneau**

J1 Mount Roberts
(corniced ridge)
J2 Perseverance
(avalanche)
J3 Mount Juneau
(avalanche and exposed
snow slopes)
J8 Sheep Creek
(avalanche)

**Sitka**
St6 Beaver Lake
(avalanche and slides)

**Skagway**
S1 Chilkoot Trail
(avalanche danger above
Sheep Camp)
S8 Denver Glacier
(avalanche towards the
end)

## OVERNIGHT TRAILS OR LONGER

**Admiralty Island**
A1 Admiralty Island Canoe
Traverse

**Juneau**
J1 Mount Roberts to J8
Sheep Creek
J18 Auke Nu to J19
Peterson Lake

**Ketchikan**
K1 Deer Mountain to K2
Mahoney Mountain
K8 Naha (cabins)

**Petersburg**
P1 Raven's Roost (ski
cabin)
P3 Petersburg Creek
(cabin)

**Skagway**
S1 Chilkoot (day-use
cabins)
S3 Upper Dewey Lake
(cabin)
S9 Laughton Glacier
(cabin)

## HISTORICAL TRAILS

**Juneau**
J2 Perseverance (Last
Chance and Silverbow
basins)
J6 Mount Jumbo (Paris
Creek)
J7 Treadwell Ditch
J8 Sheep Creek
J9 Bishop Point (Dupont)
J19 Peterson Lake
J23 Amalga-Eagle Glacier
J24 Yankee Basin

**Sitka**
St4 Totem Walk
St7 Airport Causeway

**Skagway**
S1 Chilkoot Trail
S6 Gold Rush Cemetery

**Wrangell**
W1 Wrangell City Walk
(Shakes Island)

# INDEX

3 0020 00319 7839

MARGARET PIGGOTT was born in England, where she took to the hills at an early age. In search of bigger mountains, she moved first to Canada and then to the western United States, where she climbed extensively. Her job as a physiotherapist brought her to Alaska, where she has lived now for 20 years. Currently a resident of Haines, Alaska, she travels frequently throughout the southeast part of the state as an itinerant physical therapist. Despite a busy career, she continues to hike, climb, kayak, and sled-race in the Alaskan outdoors.